25 Home Practices & Tools for Peak Holistic Health & Wellness

# THE ULTIMATE GUIDE TO
# SELF-HEALING

## VOLUME 2

25 Home Practices & Tools for Peak Holistic Health & Wellness

# THE ULTIMATE GUIDE TO
# SELF-HEALING

## VOLUME 2

# LAURA DI FRANCO

**Featuring**: Holly Alexander, Pam Bohlken, Richard W. Bredeson, Dr. Kim Byrd-Rider, Susan & Jon Cross, Laura Furey, Liz Goll Lerner, Dawne Horizons, KaNikki Jakarta, Dianna Leeder, Ronda Livingston, Kim B Miller, Dr. Lorraine Olivero-Brodeur, Susan Purvis, Lilia Shoshanna Rae, Rev. Dr. Stephanie Red Feather, Douglas Ruark, Stacey Siekman, Neelam Singh, Janette Stuart, Kristi Sullivan, Andrea R Warren, Dr. Sarah Nani Williams

Brave Healer Productions

*The Ultimate Guide to Self-Healing Vol 2*
*25 Home Practices & Tools for Peak Holistic Health and Wellness*

Laura Di Franco, MPT

# Dedication

To the men and women who stepped up to help me heal the world; thank you. The authors of these books are true healers. They understand the journey. They understand that empowering their clients to heal themselves is the biggest gift they give. They walk the path with awareness, authenticity, courage, and an indomitable spirit. I'm incredibly honored to be here among them, guiding this book project. I've pinched myself every day since it began. And this time, when that boring voice said, *who am I to do this*? I had a different answer than in the past. *Laura Di Franco is my name, and Brave Healing is my game. I'm here to change the world with my words!* This book is dedicated to every soul who helped me stand up and say that out loud with fire in my voice. I'm now helping others find their fire, and share their powerful words and voices with the world. Thank you. The ripple is real.

# Special Note to the Reader

There's something in the healing world that we call the Healing Crisis. It's a form of awareness I'd like you to know about as you dive into these pages. A healing crisis happens when we're feeling the energy of an old injury, pain or past trauma as it's coming up to be released or healed. That resistance comes up in you in the form of thoughts, sensations, feelings, emotions, and sometimes memories that don't feel good. Notice your habitual reactions to them. Sometimes it's exactly what you're having the most resistance around (words, ideas, practices, conversations, etc.) that are the biggest opportunity for healing. Skilled healers recognize this, and assist their clients through it with tools such as dialoguing, energy work, hands-on practices and modalities, and mindset and awareness coaching.

The healing crisis and your own resistance are each an opportunity to go a layer deeper. They are doors to release and relief. And sometimes, it feels so bad you think you'll die. Please know that we (author-healer-experts) get it. And we're here for you.

If you own this book, you have access to a very special private Facebook group called The Ultimate Guide to Self-Healing Community, where our author experts are hanging out to help with you questions, and live training. This is an incredible benefit to being a book owner. Make sure to take advantage of it, especially if you're stuck or have questions about what you're feeling. You're not alone. We're here to help you. Your questions will be welcomed and your concerns will be honored. You'll have a safe space to do this work of healing.

You'll get your invitation to the group at https://lauradifranco. com/ultimate-self-healing/

See you there!

# DISCLAIMER

This book offers health and nutritional information and is designed for educational purposes only. You should not rely on this information as a substitute for, nor does it replace professional medical advice, diagnosis, or treatment. If you have any concerns or questions about your health, you should always consult with a physician or other healthcare professional. Do not disregard, avoid, or delay obtaining medical or health-related advice from your healthcare professional because of something you may have read here. The use of any information provided in this book is solely at your own risk.

Developments in medical research may impact the health, fitness, and nutritional advice that appears here. No assurances can be given that the information contained in this book will always include the most relevant findings or developments with respect to the particular material.

Having said all that, know that the experts here have shared their tools, practices, and knowledge with you with a sincere and generous intent to assist you on your health and wellness journey. Please contact them with any questions you may have about the techniques or information they provided. They will be happy to assist you further!

# Contents

## Chapter 25: Hiring a Guide

### Taking Your Health to the Next Level

# Introduction

I woke up on March 20, 2020 from a dream. After days of pure panic about my entire physical therapy business being shut down in a single day during the pandemic, I'd been practicing everything I preach. *You don't know the bigger picture yet*, I thought to myself. And with a deep, full breath, *what else is possible here?*

Dwelling in that one question has served me in more ways than I can count. So that morning, I remembered to follow the feeling of possibility. I slipped out of bed, pulled my sweats on and walked into the kitchen. *You've been wanting to do this for like four years*, I heard the voice say, *why now? Because the world needs us right now*, I replied, lifting up the silver top of my MacBook and hurrying to a Facebook group where my lovely healer goddesses hang with me.

"Ladies, who wants to write a chapter with me?" I typed, "The world needs to know how to heal at home right now and we can teach them."

In 48 hours I had all 24 yeses. Five weeks later, *The Ultimate Guide to Self-Healing* was born with powerful stories and simple tools that the reader could do at home. From that morning until the very moment I type these words in volume 2, something much bigger than me has been driving this bus. All I've been doing is following orders. Being in the abundant flow in such a powerful way has solidified my knowing that when you align with joy you're an unstoppable force of good. This book is part of that energy.

In fact, what you'll read here is all pure, powerful, palpable energy from 25 expert authors. They step up into their authentic selves in their stories for you, and then they drop their expertise in the form of teaching a tool you can practice as you read. Take a moment with that same deep, full breath I took and ask yourself:

What else is possible for my healing today?

Dwell in the question. Because you might just be about to learn something that could change everything.

Another question to answer here, right up front, is why holistic healing? I mean, isn't any kind of healing great? Ask any experienced healer and they will tell you that authentic healing must be holistic. That means the incorporation and integration of mind, body, soul and spirit. Because all our wounds effect all of who we are. A physical injury always has mental, emotional and spiritual components. A mental or emotional insult always has physical components. Every single emotion you feel has a physiology in your body. To only address one aspect of you would be to miss a big part of the picture. Addressing only one part of the picture usually ends up in temporary or partial results in terms of healing.

When I put the call out to my healer friends that morning I already knew who I was asking to assist me. Aside from being badasses, these holistic healers roll with integration in mind. They know if they address your back pain, but forget to ask you about the job or loved one you lost this month, they'll miss a big opportunity to help you heal. They know if they address your back pain, but forget to tie in your entire body system into their evaluation, they'll miss another opportunity for more complete healing. And most of all they know that if they don't empower you to connect to your own inner guide, healer, and wisdom, they'll never be doing what they should to help you with the most powerful way to heal that there is; YOU!

You'll enjoy a very holistic approach on these pages and you may notice repeating themes such as a connection to the breath, enhancing your intuition, or becoming aware of what you're thinking. There are some basic, foundational principles of healing that are so key it bears repeating them. The most important thing to catch yourself saying? "I already know that." Drop into a beginner's mind, the true mark of a master, and dwell in the possibility that there might be something new about that particular topic that you haven't heard before.

Enjoy the journey!

# CHAPTER 1

# Authentic Healing
## The Awareness You Need Before You Start

### BY LAURA DI FRANCO, MPT

## My Story

What's authentic healing? Answering that one question has been the foundation of my entire journey on this planet this time around. My soul gifts, The Communicator, and Healing Love, danced in me from the beginning on tiny pages of a little blue and white polka-dotted journal.

"You have two soul gifts. Not everyone has two. Having two is a little more complicated."

When a powerful healer friend spoke to me more recently about this, the feeling of resonance around my heart center was slightly different than past moments of knowing. A vibration of validation began as a deep heartache that bubbled the remaining doubt up and out, leaving me smiling and tearing up at the Zoom screen.

"You're a powerful, full-blown channel," she continued. "The urgency you've been feeling is part of this."

More validation. "You can ask them to slow this down," she said.

*I'm not sure I want them to,* I thought. "Okay," I replied.

The urgency, like shrink-wrap around my solar plexus and heart, had tried to fool me into thinking it was a "No," as I'd often taught people in terms of listening to their intuition. But this was different. I knew it was. Yet hearing the words from someone more connected than me was important in that moment. Was I ever going to learn that I was that connected too?

"All coaches need coaches," I hear those words so many times from all the good ones. And in that moment of validation I understood that that feeling of urgency, the same one that only months earlier sent me to the lawyer's office to have my will drawn up, was the compass I'd been teaching others about. The purpose-driven fear in me was part of the language I still needed to learn, in the unique way I'm meant to learn it.

*OMG, this must mean I'm going to die soon,* was the thought in my head. *Why else would I be feeling this? How else would so much be coming through me?* I mistook the urgency for a message of "Hurry up." But it wasn't about that. It was about slowing down, opening up, and enjoying the full-on ride; the Universe trying to show me that everything I ever dreamed of was available and possible.

With that new awareness I then had a different choice. Oh, fucking awareness. If I had a nickel for every time I've uttered that word as the key to healing and happiness I'd surely be a billionaire by now. And just when you think there's nothing else to learn, guess what? The awareness shows you the next layer to heal.

Mine? Attachment to other's love as a means to my worthiness. Anyone?

Throughout my life, no matter what I did, there was never enough of that acknowledgement. School, sports, jobs, relationships, marriage, motherhood, better jobs, my own business, awards, books...I hadn't learned to give it to myself. I hadn't learned that I was the only one who could ever give that to myself in a way that would truly matter and last.

Until I did.

Thirty years as a holistic physical therapist, working with a multitude of healing modalities, each peeling a layer off, each opening a door that beckoned me to climb a step deeper and darker, into my soul, was how I stepped toward understanding how to love myself like I'd craved. And I remain in complete awe of it all today, as I craft this chapter. The awareness always gives us a choice to journey forward. The awareness always gives us a choice to move toward what feels amazing. The awareness in my life, always gives me the choice for joy, no matter how bad it feels in the moment. Always.

I've spent so many years trying not to make mistakes, or fail. Much of my journey has been trying to be a perfect good girl, to win the love of whoever was watching, or cared, or was measuring me. I tiptoed around moments being very careful not to do or say anything I'd have to apologize for later, and making sure I did and said things that would make people love me.

Holy crap that was fucking exhausting. So, I do swear in my writing. I be myself. I feel into myself and let her express, especially if it feels good, and never to harm. I prioritize my healing because when I do, the energy rides in like a surfer in the pipeline and I get to serve from an overflow. That energy is real and gets me comments like, "How do you have so much energy?" And, "It's like you're on the Audubon, I can't keep up." And, "You know Laura, it takes some stamina to roll with you."

The last one makes me smile. When I first heard that from one of my coaches, I took offense. I thought, *oh no, is that bad?* Good Girl Syndrome showing up again. Today I'm here knowing it's good. Way good. Badass good. Really, super-awesome good. Feel me? Awareness has given me this gift. Because when I choose to prioritize joy, use my awareness for that one purpose, I begin to feel the overflow. An overflow waiting for you too.

If you're my friend or someone in my family reading this you know that part of my story is moving from being a painfully shy young woman who couldn't look you in the eyes to standing at a microphone speaking brave healing out loud and healing my heart and soul as a warrior goddess. You also know that awareness is my tool. If you're a stranger to me, welcome to my world. I'm very happy you're meeting me at this stage of my game. I wasn't always playing it like you're seeing now. I fully understand that pain, in all of it's forms, is paralyzing. I fully understand that to heal, you must first feel everything. I fully understand that to feel everything, you'll have to give yourself permission to do that, and that it's difficult some days. I fully understand that you're a badass warrior for being on the journey at all, and for stepping up with a beginner's mind to learn something new. I want you to know that there is an entire community of us doing this with you. You'll never be alone as you dive within to do the sometimes impossible work of healing. I hope this book is a door to that hope, possibility, and joy for you.

Let's practice the awareness you need as you begin on this path and set yourself up for success in mind, body, and soul expansion, growth, and brave, authentic healing.

## The Tool

The Brave Healing method is a combination of body awareness and journaling. It's melding the observation of thoughts and sensations with the act of moving words from the inside to the outside onto paper, attempting not to censor what's moving through. Prolific writers know that writer's block is bullshit. The problem is you've moved out of your body and the connection to your intuition and deeper inner guide, and into your mind, and you're thinking too much.

Thinking your way through will stop you up. Feeling your way through will move you and shift the energy. And it's the energy shift we're after. With awareness you'll have a choice to think, believe and behave in ways that shift your energy toward joy. And one of the easiest ways to do that is to breathe and write.

*What you'll need:* A notebook and pen.

*What to keep in mind:* Find a place where you won't be interrupted or distracted. Leave your phone in the other room. Go to a space in your home that feels good, with great lighting, and beautiful colors, and room for you to be comfortable. If the weather is nice, find a place outdoors and allow the extra energy of nature to assist you.

To find an audio recording of the following exercise you can go to: https://lauradifranco.com/brave-book-resources/

## Body Awareness Exercise

Find a quiet place where you will not be interrupted and get into a comfortable seated position. Have your notebook and pen handy next to you. Close your eyes, and begin connecting with your body and the breath. Relax and release the head, neck, jaw, and shoulders as you breathe. Soften on each exhale. Relax and release the chest, upper back, and torso. Soften more on each exhale. Relax and release the belly, low back, hips, and butt. Soften a little more with every exhale. Finally, relax down the legs to the feet and continue to soften and let go with every exhale.

As you relax, clear your mind, and connect with the sensations of your body and the environment around you. What do you notice? What do you feel? What do you sense? With every deep inhalation and exhalation, unclench and relax your muscles. Drop your awareness and energy down into your body and just relax there and notice. Spend several minutes in this body awareness meditation, continuing to relax with every exhale.

## Writing Exercise

Now grab your pen and notebook and write as fast as you can without censoring yourself. Don't worry about punctuation, spelling, grammar or even finishing sentences. No rules, just write. Let what's coming through your mind and body in the form of the messages move through to the paper. Fill in the blank: I feel _____. Write until you feel empty, until all the words, feelings and ideas are out.

Now, take a deep breath and relax again. You may notice that during the writing process your body was tightening, or your breath halted, or changed. You may have noticed that your writing stopped flowing. That's usually because you started thinking about what you were writing and stopped just letting it flow. So take another breath, drop back down into the sensations, and if there's any more to write, continue that writing.

When you feel completely finished, take a moment to read your writing out loud to yourself. When you put the vibration of your own voice to the words and move them from your heart to your tongue, you'll feel at another level. You may even write a little bit more once you've read it out loud to yourself.

Notice what's coming up for you now. Notice any thoughts, beliefs about what you wrote, sensations in your body, or anything else coming up. Notice if your mind is trying to make the writing mean anything. Just notice. As you continue to use writing as a healing tool, it will be the awareness you practice that will be the key. And then remember, with that awareness, you have a choice to think, believe or act in a way that serves you, heals you, and moves you toward the joy.

That awareness will be the key to everything you want for your life and healing. It will be the door to freedom and joy. It will be the moment you have an opportunity to change and do something different. It will be the moment of authentic healing and the expansion of your heart. It will be a moment of learning and perspective. It will be a guide to your purpose and mission in the world.

Awareness is everything, dear reader.

And you're about to enjoy dozens more tools to help you practice. Take this chapter with you as you read the rest now. Take your notebook and pen too. As you enjoy the stories, and tools the other authors share, take notes on what you noticed, what lit you up, what you felt, where you felt it, and any inspired ideas, thoughts or other nuggets that move through you. Take a moment to notice any resistance as well. Notice what you're making things mean, and the labels you're using. Notice what your mind wants to do with certain ideas. Write down those messages or limiting beliefs. Everything you do from here on out, in the name of awareness will be a catapult for you into living as your fiercely alive whole self!

Head over to my resource link now and pick up a special journal with 25 of my favorite writing prompt questions to continue your journey. https://lauradifranco.com/brave-book-resources/

---

Laura Di Franco, MPT, is the owner of Brave Healer Productions, where she'll help you share your story, build your business and change the world with your words. With three decades of expertise in holistic physical therapy, a third-degree black belt, and ten books, she has a clear preference for being badass, and she's also the champion of entrepreneurs who want to grow their health-based practices to the next level. Her writing workshops, business strategy sessions, and online writing club are just some of the ways she helps talented professionals maximize their professional impact.

Laura's a mom of two amazing souls, an inspirational speaker, international blogger, certified content marketer, and content coordinator for Potomac Living and Bethesda Living Magazines. She's also a spoken-word poet with a passion for words that heal. You'll often find her at local open mic nights with her poet-loving friends, sipping a mojito.

If she's not writing or speaking, you'll most likely find her driving her convertible Mustang, eating dark chocolate, or bouncing to the beat at a rave. She dwells in Bethesda, Maryland, where she lives with her dogs, Reina and Leo, and dreams of moving back to her home town of San Francisco one day. www.BraveHealer.com

# CHAPTER 2

# Affirmations
## Stepping into Your Power Using Positivity

### BY JANETTE STUART

## My Story

I was diagnosed with pancreatic cancer last year. To laser focus upon my healing, I used both traditional western medicine as well as principles of thought mastery, which included affirmations.

Pancreatic cancer has grim statistics. The American Cancer Society's estimates in the United States for 2020 are:

- About 57,600 people (30,400 men and 27,200 women) will be diagnosed with pancreatic cancer.
- About 47,050 people (24,640 men and 22,410 women) will die of pancreatic cancer.

Pancreatic cancer accounts for about 3% of all cancers in the US and about 7% of all cancer deaths. It is slightly more common in men than in women.

I was inspired to create a healing journey drawing, a map, as I was preparing for major surgery; the Whipple procedure. This drawing was an amazing visual and reminder which I brought to the hospital with me. It included words of affirmation and how I wanted to feel as I focused on vibrant health. The term surgery was really scary for me even though I knew it was one of the only hopes for me to live a long and healthy life free from the disease. I reframed the word surgery and used the term "Operation Hope," which helped immensely.

My surgeon told my parents that I was one of the most positive people he had ever met. I attribute my positivity to my daily practice, which includes affirmations. I had shared my focus word of the year with him, which was flourish. I would ask myself many times a day; how can I flourish? Sometimes flourishing looked like napping, hydrating, taking an anti-nausea pill, or connecting with a loved one.

On the day of my surgery, my husband came down with shingles and had a severe case. We are now able to laugh about the timing of it, but at the time, it seemed inconceivable. I spent two weeks in the hospital and then recovered at my parent's house for an additional three weeks until I was able to eat again.

During my healing journey here are some of the affirmations I used:

- I am whole.
- I am healed.
- I am complete.
- I am loved.
- I am supported.
- I am protected.
- The Angels have my back.
- Hope is the conduit for miracles.

I am so happy to report I am healed. I am cured, I am so blessed and grateful. I just celebrated my 60th birthday. I am living each day in celebration because I am thankful for the blessing of each day, the miracle of my healing, and the glorious gift of my life. My focus word for 2020 is Celebrate. Each day, I make a list of what

I celebrated the day before. I am celebrating the big and small events with a heart full of love and gratitude.

Affirmations are important in my life. Each month, I create Angel Affirmations for The Wellness Universe, which is a platform serving the seven areas of wellness: Emotional, Environmental, Intellectual, Occupational, Physical, Social, and Spiritual. Also, for each new project or event I am involved in, I create applicable affirmations to bless my way. I use affirmations daily to help set the intention for my day, and as roadmaps for my life.

I hope my story will inspire you to try or rekindle the transformative power of affirmations as tools for stepping into your power through positivity in your life too.

## The Tool: Affirmations

### WHAT ARE AFFIRMATIONS?

They are short, powerful statements that we think, write, or speak out loud used to consciously activate positivity and transform our lives. They are declarations, a virtual blueprint, or an instruction manual of what we are consciously creating in our lives.

### WHY SHOULD I USE AFFIRMATIONS?

We are all powerful creators. The thoughts we think and the words we write and speak are magnetically calling forth those things to us. We are paving our future with these thoughts, which create our reality.

It is estimated we have about 50,000 thoughts a day, and most of them are not pretty. Often, we are extremely critical of ourselves, and we would never dream of talking to another in the way our inner critic speaks to us. We can get consumed with thoughts, worry, doubt, or unworthiness. Affirmations are the opposite of worrying. Affirmations are like prayers we offer to make things go right, and worrying is like asking for something to go wrong. They are at opposite ends of the spectrum.

We can notice these critical thoughts and choose to pay attention to the thoughts we want to further cultivate in our lives. Affirmations are like saying, "Yes, please" or "I'd like more of this" to the goodness and grace flowing in our lives.

Whatever we focus upon is the direction we head. We've seen this when we are learning to drive. If we looked at something on the side of the road, our vehicle drifted that way. What we focus upon expands. This is one of the core principles in the Law of Attraction: That Which is Like Unto Itself is Drawn.

An affirmation only needs to feel about 50% believable for it to resonate with you at a cellular level. An affirmation gives you "grow-room" for it to become your reality or for the Law of Pure Potentiality as taught by Dr. Deepak Chopra, to expand and make it your truth.

By speaking the affirmation out loud, it becomes even more powerful because you are also activating your throat chakra in the process, which further raises the vibration within your body. Repeating an affirmation out loud three times exponentially increases its effectiveness. Standing up, speaking loudly and powerfully, compounds the value of the affirmation. It allows you to step more fully into your power using the healing properties of positivity.

Affirmations that include the statement "I am" are extremely powerful. Whatever follows the "I am" becomes our truth. Let's be vigilant with the statements we think and say about ourselves. We want to select empowering statements that improve the energy vibration of our lives. We always have the choice; it's up to us. As an example, if we say, "I am tired. I am sick. I am broke. I am not worthy. I am stuck," we are calling more of that low vibration to us. These are examples of negative affirmations.

We can shift those thoughts from the previous paragraph using more energizing and empowering statements such as "I am getting the rest I need to replenish myself. I am vibrantly healthy. I am good with money. I am worthy and deserving of self-care. I am excited about..." These slight shifts have an uplifting, transformational, healing effect on the quality of our day and our lives. These are examples of positive affirmations.

Affirmations can help us all, especially during times of uncertainly. Affirmations are wonderful self-care tools that pave the way for that which we declare or affirm to be our truth. It is recommended that you craft your affirmations in the present tense and as if asking for what you do want, not for what you do not want.

Here is an example of three affirmations about the pandemic and civil unrest we are currently experiencing.

1. I am sick and tired of all the anger, pain, and suffering I see in the world. They need to do something. (Low vibration)
2. I am focusing on seeing love and light in the world. (Medium vibration)
3. I am a bright light in the world, radiating love and light in all directions. (High vibration)

In #1, use this type of affirmation if you want to experience the status quo in your reality of more sickness, tiredness, anger, pain, and suffering. (Low vibration)

In #2, use this type of affirmation if you want to improve your perception of the world reality by looking for the beauty in the situation. (Medium vibration)

In #3, use this type of affirmation if you are ready to use your thoughts and words to positively affect change in your perception of reality. This is an example of being the change you want to see in the world, as Gandhi suggests. (High vibration)

Don't worry if you have trouble moving from a low vibration type affirmation to a medium or high vibration one. Use baby steps. Just like we all learn any skill incrementally, affirmations, or changing our perception of reality requires practice.

If it's too big of a stretch to go from a low to high vibration reality, use the following language as a bridge to get you to where you want to go. The bridge language is, "I am becoming a vibrational match to..." or "I am focusing on becoming _____ " (insert the higher vibrational affirmation in the blank.)

- I am becoming a vibrational match to seeing love and light in the world.
- I am becoming a vibrational match to manifesting abundance in every area of my life.
- I am becoming a vibrational match to creating a job doing what I love, am well compensated for, and that use my talents and gifts to their fullest.
- I am focusing on becoming resilient and flexible in all areas of my life.
- I am focusing on becoming more patient with my family members and coworkers.
- I am focusing on becoming more creative by allowing myself time to paint, write, or cook.

I include affirmations in my morning practice. I refer to it as my "quiet time." It is a daily gift to myself where I set the tone of my day, spend time in devotion, and write. All of these things help fill me up with goodness and grace. You can use affirmations at any time of the day. I am a morning person, so this is my most productive time of day. Below, I will give you several affirmations you could use to start or end your day positively.

1. I am going to have a great day.
2. I am making a difference, what I do matters.
3. I am supported, protected, and safe.
4. I am surrounded by good drivers.
5. I am healthy.
6. I make good choices throughout the day.
7. I am mindful of my thoughts and actions and respond with love.
8. My contributions at work are appreciated.
9. My financial choices become easier and easier.
10. I ask for help when needed.

Just like any habit or skill, the more you use affirmations, the easier they become to implement in your life. You can also create your own affirmations for any occasion. You may want to craft some for work, your creative endeavors, a vacation, or trip, a special event such as a wedding, graduation, birthday, or party, to name a few.

I was guided to create 10 Affirmations for the authors of this book you now hold in your hands, and I'll share here with you. I believe they will bless you too on any creative project or journey you begin. You can tweak them to suit your own needs.

1. I am making a beautiful difference in the world.
2. My words matter.
3. The way I share my stories and experiences are unique gifts to give the world.
4. I let love guide my every word.
5. I am grateful for this opportunity to bless others.
6. I tap into my divine creativity and allow magic to happen.
7. I am stronger and more capable than I sometimes feel.
8. I step into the bigness and boldness of my dreams.
9. My story has never been told my way.
10. I am a brave healer.

Another way I enjoy using affirmations is to create an acrostic. No, I did not know it was a real thing until researching it for this chapter. An acrostic is a fun word composition using a word or phrases that you'll create more words or phrases from. You'll end up with some amazing results. You may have done this exercise as a child using your first name and for each letter adding an applicable word. My friend and I do this quite often with our words of the year, the alphabet, or other important words to us. Here's an example using the word affirmations:

- ♦ A = Abundance
- ♦ F = Flowing
- ♦ F = Forth

- ◆ I = Inspiring
- ◆ R = Real
- ◆ M = Magic
- ◆ A = And
- ◆ T = Transformation
- ◆ I = Influencing
- ◆ O = Our
- ◆ N = Now
- ◆ S = Statements

Now, read the whole thing as an affirmation. Here goes: Abundance Flowing Forth Inspiring Real Magic And Transformation Influencing Our Now Statements. Have fun with it. You can't get it wrong.

There are lots of affirmations available online. One of my favorite sources includes the late, great Louise Hay. For the past several years, I have been using her I Can Do It® 365 Daily Affirmations calendar, and it has truly blessed my life. This year, I am recording on the back of each daily calendar page what I celebrated that day. At the end of the year, I conduct a ritual to look back at those events documented on those slips of paper and bless the year that was as I prepare for the new year.

I hope that this chapter has sparked or renewed your interest in affirmations and that you will delight in the gift of stepping into your power using positivity.

I am grateful you took the time to read about affirmations and the benefits they can bring into your life. I have some juicy free resources for you on my website. They include a beautiful booklet/journal with various affirmations you can use again and again and a YouTube video from my channel about affirmations. I'd love to support your journey by crafting customized affirmations just for you. Let's schedule a free 20-minute affirmation call, and you'll receive 3–5 affirmations to positively impact any area of your life.

Also on my resource page is my article, Surviving Pancreatic Cancer: An Ultimate Guide for 2020 (and five tips to thrive), which you can view for yourself or send along to others who may need the gift of hope in their journey for themselves or a loved one. Visit https://www.angel-angles.com/resources

---

Janette Stuart: Emissary of Joy at Angel Angles and Well-Being and Wonder is a beacon of love, joy, peace, and gentleness. She is a #1 Best Selling author, blogger, military mom, and pancreatic cancer survivor who uses the gift of her words and positivity to assist others in embracing their divinity using tools such as her series of devotionals called "On a Path of Joy."

As an angelic practitioner, she shares goodness and grace and the healing beauty of nature frequently in her work to inspire others. She has developed an inspirational card deck called "Love Notes from The Divine" and is co-creator of "Words of Wisdom Guidance Cards" and shares daily messages of love and encouragement on social media. Janette and her friend, Becky Wilbur, have a venture called Well-Being and Wonder and host live events to encourage others to embrace self-care and ways to improvise, adapt, and overcome life's challenges.

Janette lives in the San Francisco Bay Area with her husband Mark of 37 years and their boxer dog Spike who rescued them seven years ago. She has a grown son who is proudly serving in the United States Coast Guard and is one of her biggest joys in life. She retired in 2015 from a career in finance and human resources with 36 years of service and joyfully now does the work of her soul daily. Janette loves cooking, being out in nature, writing, and has an impressive collection of stationery, pens, and journals. Some of her most requested recipes are Asian Chicken Salad, Cinnamon Rolls, and Sticky Toffee Pudding.

Connect with Janette here:

Facebook at Angel Angles with Janette Stuart, https://www.facebook.com/AngelAngles11/

Facebook at Well-Being and Wonder, https://www.facebook.com/WellBeingandWonder/

Facebook Group Angel Circle of Gratitude, https://www.facebook.com/groups/191937398373942/

Website, https://www.angel-angles.com

Website, https://www.wellbeingandwonder.com

Email, janette@angel-angles.com

# CHAPTER 3

# Intuition
## How To Trust Your Gut

### BY DR. LORRAINE OLIVERO-BRODEUR, DNP, FNP-BC

## My Story

I was around seven years old, sitting at my kitchen table, watching the evening news on our little black and white TV. On that day, they featured a segment on "medicine men and women" who were discovered living in remote villages in the high Andes. What struck me was that these people lived away from modern civilization and were able to survive off of the land. Their "healers/doctors" wore colorful ponchos and used plants as medicine, along with spiritual practices to care for the health and well-being of their community. Although at the time, I did not understand the details of exactly who they were *energetically*, their presence spoke to me at a depth of "knowing" which literally brought me to my knees, as I cried holding my heart.

I recall feeling tremendous gratitude for their wisdom teachings and understood, from a place of "no words," that this was my tribe. As I knelt on the floor, I was quickly brought back to reality by my mother yelling, "What is wrong with you? Get up off the floor!" At that moment, I understood my path. I also understood that I would have to walk it alone.

At seven years old, I became an explorer of the truth.

I loved being in the woods, amongst the trees, and sitting quietly at the lake. I listened to the sounds of Pachamama (Mother Earth), for I inherently knew that she would guide me. In the stillness of the lake, I learned to ask myself soulful questions and would find that the answers would quickly appear from my gut. I suddenly knew I was in training, for this was a *tool* I was meant to master.

I read every book on health and medicine that my library had, however, I couldn't find any books about the colorful poncho-wearing medicine people I saw on TV. Instead, I continued to explore the woods and listened to the wisdom of the plants and trees. I was amazed at how I would *feel* what they had to say. I knew my path was that of the *healer,* however, my gut told me it had to be beyond the traditional sense.

As I grew older, I continued to seek the wisdom of Pachamama, since the books were not necessarily giving me the information that I was looking for. I learned to trust my energetic self, from the place of "my gut," to continue to guide me. I enrolled in college with a major in Pre-Med/Sports Medicine. There I learned the importance of nutrition and physical movement. I dove into those teachings and began to train to become a bodybuilder, as a means to understand and experience how transformation can occur with proper food and exercise.

Soon thereafter, at the age of 20 years old, another layer of my journey appeared in the form of a book! It was called *Hands of Light* by Barbara Ann Brennan. When I started to read her book, I was like, *I'm not crazy, it is possible that I can heal from my hands!* For as long as I can remember, I felt an *energy* radiate from my hands. I would play with it like a ball, moving the distance of my hands in and out as I experienced that I could make this energetic ball really small or even expand it around me. I would love to "sit" within my energetic ball in the woods and be still, as I listened to the words of guidance that would come to me.

If someone wasn't feeling well, I would gently place my hands on them with the intention of removing whatever was ailing them.

They would say, "Thanks so much, I feel better now!" Of course, I thought that they were joking because, *how can my hands do THAT?* It's not like I ever read *that* in a book or heard so from another person, that *healing* can come from your hands.

This newfound confirmation of the existence of *energy healing* catapulted my transformational journey of higher consciousness and awareness, as I studied various ancient traditional wisdom and healing practices. I continued my traditional college education that lead me to receive a clinical doctorate from Columbia University as a *Doctor of Nursing Practice* (which is a Primary Care Practitioner with a deep understanding of Preventative and Functional Medicine).

For over 25 years, I have actively walked the path of both a traditional Primary Care Practitioner and Holistic Integrative Lifestyle Medicine Practitioner. Practicing in *both worlds* has allowed me to gain a unique eagle perspective of how to create ultimate health, wellness, and vitality. I genuinely understand the importance of consciously living a balanced lifestyle, through all dimensions of one's BE-ing (mind, body, soul, spirit, space), in order to prevent *dis-ease*.

I have such gratitude for my journey of over 30 years of exploration, study, and practice in these ancient spiritual wisdom and healing traditions, interwoven with conventional modern medicine. For this unique fusion has given me the opportunity to become the healer that I have always envisioned to be. As a result, of what I consider to be my life's work, I, along with Rich Brodeur, co-created a new complementary paradigm to western medicine called *Aquarian Medicine*—an exclusive multidimensional holistic integrative lifestyle system intended to navigate the 21st century.

Oh, and if you were wondering who those "medicine men and women" in the colorful ponchos were? They are the direct descendants of the Inka called Q'ero's; highly respected indigenous people known as the keepers of the ancient wisdom and spiritual practices of the Incas. Their "medicine men and women" are called Paqo (considered to be a combination of priest, shaman, healer, and mystic). One of my greatest honors was to be initiated into the lineage of these shamans and to be taught their ancient wisdom teachings through my mentor Dr. Alberto Villoldo.

As a side note, with all that I have studied and experienced throughout the years, I chuckle when I hear these incredible ancient wisdom teachings and practices labeled as "alternative." How can teachings that have been around for thousands of years be considered "alternative" when compared to "modern" medical practices? As I write this, modern science is beginning to now understand and respect the knowledge that the shaman, gurus, yogis, and mystics have discovered over millennia.

For example, for thousands of years, the indigenous prophecies of the Inka, the Hopi, and the Maya spoke of this "time to come," a time where the world would end as we know it and a new species of human would give birth to itself. The ancient Vedic scriptures refer to this time as the "Aquarian Age," thought to have begun on 11/11/2011. Modern science refers to this time as the "Sixth Mass Extinction," which began in December 2012. Regardless of the exact moment in time the "Age of Aquarius" began, it is quite clear that we have now entered in that "time to come," as evidenced by a shift toward globalization and increased awareness, as we transition into the Aquarian Age. It has been said that all humanity will experience a shift that is mental and spiritual, as well as social and economic.

We see this to be true with the global coronavirus pandemic of 2020, as many people approach it with confusion, anxiety, fear, and daydream. The Vedic scriptures spoke of how our minds will awaken to increased thoughts and sensations both consciously and subconsciously.

Therefore, I believe there is no better time than now to teach you the first healing tool that Pachamama taught me. The tool of *How to Trust Your Gut*. By learning how to access your inner compass, you will experience direct access to your Neutral Mind, which is the intuitive voice of your soul. When you operate from this place, you will understand the direction and manner by which you can navigate and contribute to the world in this new age.

> "There is no greater healer than you.
> There is no greater guru than you."
>
> -Dr. Lorraine Olivero-Brodeur

## The Tool

### WHAT YOU WILL NEED:

Just your authentic SELF.

The beauty of this intuitive tool is that once you become familiar with how to use your gut, you will find that you can consciously call upon it anywhere, any time, and in a moment's notice. However, for purposes of this instruction, I will break down each of the steps so that you can gain a clear understanding and conscious experience of how this works.

### HOW DO YOU DO IT?

Remember, you are born with an intuitive "knowingness"- gut instinct. How many times have you said, "*I had a gut feeling...*" It is not a coincidence that this term is in our common day vernacular.

Therefore, the purpose of this exercise is to remind you HOW to trust your gut instinct in just four steps. Let's begin.

You'll find a video version of How to Trust Your Gut written below at https://aquarianmedicine.com/brave-book-resources/.

1.   **Step One:** Sit comfortably with a straight spine, in either a chair or in Easy Pose (sitting straight and cross-legged). Sitting with a straight spine acts as a central channel of energy for your nervous system. I have found that this allows for easier transmission to access your gut-brain connection.

2.   **Step Two:** Gently close your eyes and place your hands over your second chakra (located in your lower abdomen below your navel). Focusing on your breath, inhale through your nose for a count of four. Hold your inhale for a count

of four. Then exhale through your nose for a count of four. Hold your exhale out for a count of four. Repeat two more times.

3. **Step Three:** With continued awareness of your second chakra, ask yourself a simple *Yes* or *No* question. For example: Think of a random name (other than your own) and ask yourself, "Is my name _____, Yes or No? Next, think of *your* name and ask yourself, "Is my name _____, Yes or No?

   Note how quickly your "Yes" or "No" answer presents. So quickly, in fact, that your answer of "Yes or No" presents two thirds into your asking yourself the question. *THAT is your Gut Instinct!*

   Once you are "in tune" to your gut, continue to ask yourself any questions that you would like guidance on. Allow the answers to present automatically, with no judgment. You'll find that your answers usually present in one or two words within a matter of two seconds.

4. **Step Four:** Once you have your answer, check in with your heart. Does your answer resonate with your heart? *Yes or No*? If the answer is "Yes," then you have your answer! If the answer is "No," that means your subconscious "mind" is trying to interfere. Simply check in with your gut again and repeat the above steps.

## HOW DOES THIS WORK?

Throughout my studies, I have found *gut intuition* to be a common denominator as one of the core operating tools that shaman and yogis have used for thousands of years. Western medicine is now beginning to appreciate the complexity of the interconnection of the gut, brain, and, more recently, the gut microbiome (which is made up of bacteria, archaea, fungi, and viruses that live in the gut). As an interesting side note, only 10% of our cells are actually "human." The other 90% is microbiota.

A primordial connection exists between your brain and your gut. Your "gut instinct" comes from a place of intuitive knowing and stillness, that requires "no thought," other than the question that you wish to ask it or the *feeling* that you get.

Scientific research has validated this finding through the physical presence of chemicals, hormones, and an extensive network of 50-100 million neurons found in the lining of your gut, referred to as the enteric nervous system (ENS) or "second brain." This superhighway, known as the gut-brain axis, continually provides feedback between both ends regarding the state of your emotion, health, digestion, and even the way you think.

Therefore, that "gut feeling" you experience is a direct reflection of your emotion, picked up by the nerve fibers of your vagus nerve. Interestingly, 90% of the signals picked up by the vagus nerve travel directly from the *gut to the brain*. However, only 10% of signals run in the opposite direction from the brain to the gut. Therefore, next time you have that *gut feeling* that you *should or shouldn't do something*, you may want to trust it!

## WHY SHOULD YOU "TRUST YOUR GUT"?

When you learn how to trust your gut, you access your *Guru* within. Your Guru is the inner teacher that empowers you to listen to *your* wisdom and truth, establishing deep roots within your mind that you can access whenever you need guidance. This is important because when you lead from your gut intuition, you access a part of your brain, known as the "Neutral Mind," that will guide you on how to move forward, without the influence and projection of others to define your path.

Numerous research studies from cognitive neuroscientists have shown that we are only 5% consciously aware of what is in our mind (thoughts, feelings, beliefs, emotions, actions), the other 95% lays dormant in our unconscious mind. When you act from the place of your gut, you access that 5% conscious mind, that allows you to operate from a place of empowerment and truth, as opposed to a place of fear. "Fear" that is dictated by past stories, events, and limiting beliefs that have unconsciously owned and defined you, not allowing you to move forward in life for fear of a repeat performance.

Yoga teaches us that your "higher mind or higher consciousness" consists of three Functional Minds– Positive Mind, Negative Mind, and Neutral Mind. Your mind thinks, acts, and feels differently in each aspect. Within an incredibly short period of time, your mind has the ability to analyze all that you encounter, so short in fact that it can't even be measured. This is called *intuition*.

When you trust your gut intuition, you access your Neutral Mind that allows you to speak from a place of stillness, that is in direct alignment with your soul. When you speak from your gut, it processes everything negative and positive then responds from the Neutral Mind to express you. This action leads to the fulfillment of you and your highest self.

"The intuitive mind is a sacred gift, and the rational mind is a faithful servant. We have created a society that honors the servant and has forgotten the gift."
–Albert Einstein

## HOW CAN YOU IMPROVE ACCESS TO YOUR GUT INTUITION?

This topic is a complete book in itself, however for the purpose of fine-tuning this tool, it is important to understand that most dis-ease of modern living begins in your gut and is a direct reflection of your diet and lifestyle choices.

On a daily basis, we are exposed to toxins in the form of over 81,000 chemicals and preservatives in our food, water, air, and environment. Research has shown that as a result of this toxic exposure, imbalances within your gut microbiome can occur that cause damage to the gut-brain connection. Unfortunately, I see the results of toxin exposure every day in my Primary Care Practice. Mental and emotional stress triggers physical responses that affect the gut, such as various types of digestive disease and autoimmune issues. Meanwhile, disturbances in your microbiome can affect the functioning and health of the brain, such as depression, anxiety, mental fog, and sleep disturbance.

I also see evidence of the potential to reverse *dis-ease* from my Aquarian Medicine™ practice. With the utilization of various Aquarian Medicine™ lifestyle tools, my clients are able to create restorative health and vitality through conscious and balanced living. An example of some practices that I use with my clients to help enhance their gut-brain connection is:

1. Meditation—This incredible ancient tool allows you to get in touch with your soul to help build your intuition.

2. Nutrition—Eliminating inflammatory and toxic foods, such as sugar, processed foods, genetically modified organisms (GMO's), gluten, grains, dairy, artificial sweeteners, and refined vegetable oils is the main goal when attempting to reset and balance the gut microbiome. Eating primarily an organic plant-based diet is the general recommendation.

3. Mindful movement—Such as yoga, pilates and weight-based exercises.

Lastly, *practice*!

Please be patient with yourSELF. Expect that the first few times that you attempt this exercise, your mind will question it ALL! This is a normal response. Now it's possible that you may already know how to *trust your gut,* and if so, awesome! However, most people come from a place of looking for validation to the truth *outside* of their body as opposed to *withIN*. Trust that all the answers that you will ever need to know live within you. By *trusting your gut,* you are sure to get the answers to your deepest questions, where YOU become the author of your own story and live the life that YOU dream!

---

Dr. Lorraine Olivero-Brodeur is a Co-Founder of Aquarian Medicine™, a proprietary multidimensional Holistic Integrative Lifestyle Medicine System intended to navigate the 21$^{st}$ century.

As a Primary Care Practitioner for over 25 years, Dr. Lorraine understands the importance of her patients obtaining balance "with-IN" so that "dis-ease" does not present itself either physically, mentally, emotionally and/or spiritually. Her quest to learn how to achieve this *balance* has been the driving force behind 30+ years of continued study and certification in numerous ancient wisdom and healing practices of energy medicine, indigenous shamanic medicine, ancient Vedic healing arts, Ayurveda, Kundalini Yoga, herbology, sound vibration, meditation, martial arts and leading-edge conventional medical practices in primary care medicine, nutrition, neuroscience, and biology. This evolution of continued study has led her and Rich Brodeur to co-create Aquarian Medicine.

In her spare time, Dr. Lorraine loves to spend time with her family and fur babies making precious moments. She enjoys daily research on exploring the most innovative conventional findings in nutrition, neuroscience, higher consciousness, and biology of the body. She lives and works in the suburbs of New York City and offers in-person and digital distance Aquarian Medicine™ consultations and Aquarian Shamanic Energy Medicine sessions. You can connect with Dr. Lorraine Olivero-Brodeur at www.AquarianMedicine.com

# CHAPTER 4

# De-Cluttering
## How to Clear Mental and Physical Spaces to Manifest Creativity

### BY KANIKKI JAKARTA
The First African American Poet Laureate of Alexandria, Virginia

DO NOT think of a dolphin. You did it, didn't you? You thought of a dolphin! Chances are when someone asks you not to think of a thing, you think of that thing. I presented the dolphin to you because studies reveal that marine mammals can remember their friends for twenty years. So think of a dolphin, and don't forget to remember that you have the power not to forget.

## My Story

"My clothes have expired!" I exclaim periodically when coming home from work, or let me be honest, when coming home from anywhere. My thoughts are that clothes are for outside. So, when I have made it safely inside my home, I kick them off as soon as they have served their purpose of being on stage with me or at work with me. I have a busy schedule, personally and professionally. I noun and verb the titles wife and mother. I am a full-time Human Resource Specialist and a full-time Performance Poet who just happens to be holding the title of the First African American Poet Laureate of Alexandria, Virginia. By day, I hire people. By night, I inspire people. On the day that Laura Di Franco texted me asking me what I would write, I was sitting on my bed looking at everything I had worn the days before in my room overflowing in a basket next to my window, reflecting from my full-length mirror. I looked up at my reflection staring back at me, and the basket of clothes that I could see twice. I could hear my mother Antoinette's voice, "Cleanliness is next to Godliness," she used to tell me. I quickly replied that I would write about decluttering, decluttering the space in your mind, and decluttering your physical space. If cleanliness is next to Godliness is a fact, I wasn't sitting next to God.

We have all done it, haven't we? Don't leave me out on a lonely limb. To plant this metaphorical tree of life, we all have planted in hopes of bearing fruits, but some of those fruits don't get plucked, and when those fruits fall, we seemingly never have the opportunity to pick them up. I'm often interviewed; the interviewer will sometimes ask me, "How are you doing this?" "This," meaning everything from being a successful wife and mother, and working a success at a nine-to-five, and having a successful professional poetry career. I tell them, "I am not." Because the truth is, my mother taught me the saying, "If you fail to plan, you plan to fail." I took it as a life mantra to follow. I am a great planner, but sometimes my husband gets neglected, sometimes my child gets neglected, sometimes my writing gets neglected, and sometimes when I'm at work I'm thinking about how my writing is being neglected because I am working a nine-to-five. Periodically, clutter builds up around me, and it blocks my creativity. That's when I channel my grandmother, Ruth Ola Mae, who taught me how to clean. It is my pleasure to offer you; how clearing your mental and physical space will manifest your creativity! (Insert applause)

## ENERGY

Let's start with energy because you will need the strength and vitality required for sustained physical and mental activity. The definition of energy explained here is what is needed to clear your physical space. If you design a space to create, that space holds the energy of creativity. My great uncle Daniel Cooley built a space for his wife and my aunt Mary separate from their home. She and her daughter Denise were seamstresses when I was a child. When I was growing up, my aunt Denise made a lot of my clothes. In their separate space, she made beautiful clothing and was an inspiration to me. The clothes hanging on the walls and the fabric were full of life and creative energy. I am a writer, and although they were seamstresses, I can relate to their creativity space. Now that we know clothes hold energy, can we agree that cluttered clothing and other things that are cluttered in your home hold energy as well? What kind of energy are the things that are cluttering your space holding in your life?

## OVERWHELMED

Bury or drown beneath a huge mess.

Let's change this definition a bit and say that thinking of clearing your physical clutter is overwhelming, and your creativity is buried down beneath a huge mess. Guess what? You have the energy to clear it all.

# The Tool

### *Here is your tool:*

Your mindset is the tool that you need to succeed. Change your mind, change your reality.

"If you can't change the people around you,
change the people around you."

"If you change the way you look at things,
the things you look at will change."
– Wayne Dyer

## AFFIRMATIONS

Train your mind with positive thoughts of affirmation. An affirmation is an action or process of affirming something or being affirmed. You have the power to affirm yourself. Remember our metaphorical tree of life? Well, consider this, what you water will grow. So if you water negative energy, you'll have a negative lifestyle. But on the other hand, if you water positivity, you will grow that as well.

Say aloud: "I have the birthright of abundance." The words that you speak after, "I am…" are what you create for yourself. You have the power to create something beautiful. Why not start with yourself? Try: "I am creating an organized, successful life for my family and me."

It does not matter if you clean everything. Until you have a mindset that is focused on being organized, clean, and clear of clutter, you will go back to old patterns.

Let us first clear our minds of clutter. Examine how much time you spend on social media, watching television, and talking to friends and family members. How do you feel after you've read social media posts, watched a series, or talked to those whom you talk to on a regular basis? Do you visit social media and hold on to what you've read about someone else's life? Do you feel empowered by the television shows you watch? Are your friends and family members solution-based people, or are they unloading their problems on to you? What are you carrying in your mind that is not your business and not your problem to solve? More importantly, does spending your time doing these things take away from the time you could be clearing and organizing your own space in your mind and your reality? What could you have created if you weren't consumed with these things or people? Repeat after me, "Grown people are not my responsibility." Okay, now that you know that, you can get on with your life and keep it together.

## PURPOSE, SENTIMENTAL, AND BEAUTY

Every single thing in your home should be something of beauty that you are admiring when looking at it, such as photos or paintings. Other things should serve a specific purpose. I know that we're sentimental beings, so we must keep sentimental items, but be careful to make sure that those sentimental things also serve a purpose. I will tell you that I still had a robe that my very first boyfriend gave me when I was a teenager. "Why, KaNikki?" Well, it held sentimental value, being the first thing someone outside of my family gifted to me. Honey child, I didn't need it! What purpose was it serving? I can remember what it looked like. Those things that have no purpose but hold sentimental value can also hold a memory when we do not have the physical space for it.

## A PLACE

Everything in your home must have a place. The coffee maker has a place, shoes have a place, and even a fingernail clipper has a place. If there is no place, you do not have space for it. This means you're going to have to donate or toss out many things. Get your trash and donation bags together. It's time to make space and a place for everything.

### Pick a target:

A table
A dresser
A cabinet
A closet
A drawer

### *Pick a time and a time limit:*

You didn't clutter in one day, so you're not going to be able to de-clutter in one day. So, now that you're not on social media, on the phone, or watching TV, and being about the business of minding your business, you have an hour to declutter. You will not know how much space you have until you rid your home of things that do not hold beauty, sentimental value, or a useful purpose.

Once you've gotten rid of things, you can organize and make places for all of your items and this way you do not waste time searching for things. After all, we know time does not wait!

My grandmother, Ruth Ola Mae, taught me to clean from corner to corner. Most things end up in a corner, and if you clear them out first, you have made a great start. Clean the corners and then clean under: Under the bed, under the couch, under the table. Then work your way to the middle. Before you know it, everything has been cleaned.

When your home is clutter-free, and you've freed up some time, you can now be a creator. I am a writer and a believer that if you create a physical, creative space, that space will always hold the creative energy needed to manifest.

For example: Let us build a physical writing space:

- Colored pens to express a mood
- Pencils in case I want to erase
- Pencil sharpener so that I do not have to leave the space to sharpen
- Loose paper, blank notebooks, and journals
- A light that adjusts from dim to bright
- A Comfortable chair
- A table with wheels that lock so that I can write in different positions
- A throw blanket in case I get cold
- Sticky notes to brainstorm
- Laptop

- Power strip
- Photos of me performing on the wall
- Framed awards on the wall
- Inspirational painting

Your space does not have to look identical to mine. Whatever it is that makes you comfortable and gets you into the mood of writing is what you need.

Now that your mind and space are clear, how do you possess your writing process? Download a free guide of steps to start writing on my website: www.kanikkij.com/clear-create Search around, I offer writing workshops monthly, find the one that fits your interest.

Whether your mission is to create clothing, create books, or create something entirely different, you are the author of your own story; you create the narrative. Being alive is all about making that dash count between the time you were birthed and the time that you transition.

Think of a clean, organized home, and a mind clear and focused. You did it, didn't you? You thought of yourself being able to manifest your creativity with an organized home and a clear mind. See, telling you to think of a thing also works. Thoughts become things, and you have the power not to forget.

Now, think yourself into a positive life.

KaNikki Jakarta is the First African American Poet Laureate of Alexandria, Virginia. She is an award-winning performance poet who has toured the United States and the United Kingdom. She is the author of three novels, two poetry collections, a memoir, and a short-story poetry collection entitled ALABAMA GIRL, VIRGINIA WOMAN. She hosts #KaNikkiHarmony Open Mic Night every first Monday at Busboys and Poets, Virginia. She facilitates a Quarterly Workshop entitled: WRITE LIKE A WOMAN in Alexandria, Virginia, and various monthly publishing and writing workshops virtually. She presents POETS AND PLATFORM under the umbrella of a weekly, online woman-led artistic experience entitled KEEP THE MIC ON, where she is the co-founder.

If you think that something she says on the mic might change your life, you're probably right.

| | |
|---|---|
| Website: | https://www.kanikkij.com |
| For Booking: | Contact Kecia James at greatpublishing@yahoo.com |
| Facebook: | https://www.facebook.com/kanikkij |
| Twitter: | https://www.twitter.com/kanikkij |
| Instagram: | https://www.instagram.com/kanikki_j |

# CHAPTER 5

# Money Healing
## Using Magic Money Mantras for Total Transformation

### BY HOLLY ALEXANDER

## My Story

I was raised by well-meaning parents who had, shall we say, some interesting ideas and beliefs around money. While they were well-educated professionals earning an abundance of money, there was an underlying scarcity I felt and saw and, therefore, unconsciously adopted. My father would spend hours obsessing about money, many times spending more than we could afford, and then freak out when he was unable to pay our regular bills. My mother would quietly use the grocery money to buy other things we needed and then become angry and resentful she had to sneak around. Money was abundant and, along with it, came an abundance of negative emotions and fighting. It seemed as quickly as it would come in, it would go out. It was no surprise the same was true for me and my money situation as soon as I was out on my own as a young adult. These beliefs and behaviors, which I rightfully thought were perfectly normal, were a part of my operating system. I didn't realize until a few years into my adult life that I had adopted their beliefs as part of my day-to-day operating system and drove my behavior. I, too, would obsess over money: *how much did I have? How much was I expecting? What bills needed to be paid? How much would I have leftover? How much was my debt?* It was awful—I was driven by fear and dread, bordering on panic, all the time. No sooner would I receive money than I would distribute it and, rather than being grateful I had received, I was resentful I hadn't received more. Does this sound at all familiar?

Thankfully, I also had other money models. My bosses and friends were interesting case studies for me around money. I observed that their attitudes and beliefs about money were different from mine by how they handled and talked about money. I was open to something new and different, and I observed them quietly, noticing big and little differences. They lived in abundance: they lived in beautiful homes, described trips and vacations, wore expensive clothes, and never stressed about money. They talked about money in positive ways, and said things like, "There's always more where that came from!" Where I was concerned, they were generous. They paid for meals, gave excellent gifts, and when it came time for me to get a raise, I always got the maximum amount. There was a difference in how we felt about money. It wasn't long before I started to question what I felt, thought, and believed.

It didn't take me long to discover I liked and desired the finer things in life. As luck would have it (or as I call it, divine intervention), several teachers crossed my path and allowed me to uncover, examine, and eventually heal my wealth wounds. It was a long, multi-year process I wish had been shorter for me, and hopefully, with what I share with you here, you'll make a fast and smooth transition into abundance—because if I had known then what I know now, that's what I would have done. Now, you can.

## The Tool

My intention in this chapter is to share three Money Magnetizers with you to open your mind to the prosperity, wealth, and abundance that can be yours. It can provide you with a transformational tool so you can have your money healing within the shortest period possible, and begin to experience a life filled with all of the money you could ever want or need. If you want to go deeper into this work, you can find my complete philosophy in the Magic Money Book Series. Grab the first book as my gift in my bio at the end of this chapter.

Allow me to explain what a Money Magnetizer is: it is your inner money setting, such that when you "turn it on," money begins to flow to you—as if by magic. I believe we all have these internal settings, yet we have never been told they exist, and we sure as heck haven't learned how to activate them! In my early twenties, as I began to search the bookshelves (first the traditional ones, then the spiritual ones). I found those who had gone before me and uncovered what some have called secrets. But if someone knows about them and shares them, they aren't secrets, right? Yet, they aren't widely known (which to me is a bummer). I figured if one person can use them and they work, why couldn't I use them and they work for me?

## Money Magnetizer #1:

Your bounty plus gratitude equals abundance. The first Money Magnetizer is to recognize that there is more than enough of everything you want and need, everywhere present around you, at all times. Your job is to look for it, recognize it, and give thanks for it.

Said more traditionally, you turn on the part of your brain known as the reticular activating system (or RAS) that notices things. If I tell you to, as Pam Grout does in *E-Squared: Nine Do-It-Yourself Energy Experiments That Prove Your Thoughts Create Your Reality*, look for a beige Volkswagen Jetta, sooner or later, you're going to see one! Why? Because you've told your brain, "Look for this! Notice it when you see it!" Your RAS turned on and tuned in, and is on the lookout for what you tell it to find.

Why not, from this moment forward, look for and find an abundance of everything you want? It's there just waiting for you to notice it (and claim it, but I'm getting ahead of myself). As trees are abundant, as are grains of sand (and yes, beige Volkswagen Jettas), there is an abundance of money in the world just waiting for you, my sweet friend, and the only person standing in the way of it flowing to you...is you.

The next piece of the puzzle is this: once you notice the abundance, throw in a massive helping of gratitude. Gratitude is a maximizer for your maximizer! Seeing abundance plus gratitude expedites the flow to you. When I turned my thoughts to gratitude, I began to experience more and more wealth. The more grateful I was, the more I had to be grateful for—it was terrific!

Can we agree you have an abundance of things to be grateful for, and ample opportunity to express your gratitude? Good, remember: bounty plus gratitude equals abundance.

## Money Magnetizer #2:

Money flows to those who respect it. Our default setting is to be attracted to anyone and anything that treats us with respect. Conversely, anyone or anything negative, rude, or disrespectful causes us to go away. Money is energy and reacts the same way—when it is treated with love, honor, and respect, it comes to us, stays, and brings its friends. *Smile.* When treated with disrespect, neglect, or even contempt, it goes away and goes away fast.

When avalanches of abundance have flowed into your life before today, what happened to them? Have you been grateful? Have you given some away to keep the flow going? Have you put some away for later? Have you gratefully had fun with your money and recorded the memory? Money that is shared, saved, and enjoyed feels valued, and you can rest assured when you treat money as though it is appreciated, more is on its way to you.

Alternatively, as you've received money, have you squandered it? Misused it? Wasted it? Condemned or criticized it? Perhaps you've gotten mad at it because it didn't come as often or as much as you needed it?

Oh, and lest you think I'm pointing the finger at you, I'm merely pointing out what I was doing before I "got it." But if I'm describing you, that's okay. When we know better, we do better, right? YES.

Substitute money for a job, friend, spouse, or anything else—if you treated anything or anyone else (yourself?!) the way you may have been handling money, is it a wonder you don't have more than you want or need? When I started treating money with the respect it deserves, it began to come to me in magical ways, expected and unexpected, from all points of the Universe. Here's a short lesson in respecting your money: any time you receive money, have a plan for every dollar. In *Advanced Magic Money*, I share exactly how I allocate my streams of income. In one sentence, here it is: I give, save, spend, and invest in pre-determined percentages—and as soon as the money comes in, I exercise my plan. Pre-determining your plan goes a long way toward showing your money you respect it.

One more quick tip to magnetize money: have fun with your money! Even if, right now, you are flat broke (or in debt up to your eyeballs), take one percent of your income (or even $10) and buy yourself something wonderful. Or, do something with that money that brings you great joy. Remember, money is energy. Fun and joy are high vibration emotions, the same feelings that are most inclined to cause more money to flow to you.

But wait, there's more! Money Magnetizers #1 and #2 are just the beginning, and you can do them as quickly and as easily as you take your next breath. This next Money Magnetizer is just as simple and as easy, and it accelerates the effectiveness of the first two.

## Money Magnetizer #3:

What you talk about comes about. I believe with every cell of my being that "to speak is to create." I learned from Dr. Catherine

Ponder about affirmations in her many books. She taught me to say what I wanted and only what I wanted—words are substance, and we can speak what we want to bring into existence and come to us.

The ancient Egyptians believed in the power of the spoken word, and "what flows from your mouth happens" and "that which you speak comes into being." Once I realized this truth, I stopped saying anything and everything I didn't want to bring into my life (or anyone else's!) and started blessing every situation as good. I believe, and I say every single day, "Only good can come from this." No matter how awful the case, or how hard the challenge, I say, "Only good can come from this." Sometimes it takes a few hours, other times it can be weeks or months. As I persevere, believing wholeheartedly good is on the way, it eventually shows up! (Side note: the longer it takes to come, the bigger and better it is!)

If there is a situation in your life or the world, you want to change, watch your words, and speak only what you want to happen! But while you're at it...

## Set Yourself Free for a Mega-Money Healing and Effortless Prosperity

This next part is my favorite—and for those of you who have, up until now, believed money only comes to those who work hard and long hours under less-than-ideal circumstances, allow me to blow your mind (in a good way):

Success may be as much as 98% inner preparation and 2% outer action.

Yes, you read that correctly! Your money healing starts and ends with your thoughts, words, and actions (your money actions). You do not have to strain and strive; you can think and speak what you want, respect your money, and begin to expand quickly into a life of complete and utter abundance and prosperity. The truth is that these three Money Magnetizers are all you need to handle that 98%! I've always joked that my 2% is going to the mailbox to grab the checks!

## Your Tool for Money Healing and Transformation: Magic Money Mantras

If "to speak is to create," it is important to speak only what you do want and never what you don't. If you've been guilty of chastising your money, flip the switch and begin to praise it! Welcome it into your life like a long lost friend who has shown up with chocolate and wine!

You can conjure up money in abundance in your life, while simultaneously healing your ideas and beliefs around money, by speaking what you want into existence. Affirmations have gotten a lot of press (and some criticism), but the truth about them is proven. They work, and they work like a charm! And get this, when you speak passionately and consistently about something, you can speed up your results by as much as 80% (who doesn't want fast results, especially when it comes to money?). As I mentioned before, success can be as much as 98% inner preparation—a lot of it accomplished through our thoughts (mental pictures) and our spoken words.

Through affirmations, you can completely transform your relationship with money and experience a money healing faster, better, and in more significant amounts than you may right now believe is possible.

Instead of calling them affirmations, I call them mantras. Mantras are defined as sacred utterances holding spiritual power. Mantras are words or phrases spoken out loud in repetition. I know from experience when I use them, they work. From the time I started using them (and I've continued for almost thirty years) until today, I have realized results naturally and often faster than I ever thought possible. I've used mantras to heal my limiting beliefs around money and expand my beliefs around money.

A simple formula for synchronously healing your beliefs about money, while manifesting more (much more!) into your life is this: Take a statement, your new mantra, that expresses the life, abundance, and wholeness you want to experience, and declare it repeatedly. In other words, name your good to claim your good! Your statement can be scripture or some other statement of abundance that appeals to you. It does not matter that, at first, you do not believe it, or cannot see how it can come true. When you persistently affirm it anyway, even though you don't quite mentally accept it, you will find that your affirmations have power. You will experience results rapidly and peacefully and with almost no effort. If your beliefs are the result of decades of thought and experience, remember this: the regular, persistent drop of water will wear away the hardest stone. Your repeated mantra will bring results to you as quickly as within twenty-four hours, and as you persist in using them, it will cause you to experience more abundance more rapidly than you have ever seen before. Simply set aside time every day to speak your mantra for at least five minutes--or as much as an hour. Over and over, repeat your mantra. You can say it out loud as few as fifteen times, or as many as two thousand times in a row or more. It depends on how quickly you want to see results! I say my mantras while I'm in the shower, walking my dog, and folding laundry. I say them when I'm running errands, before making important phone calls, or when I'm perhaps not-so-patiently waiting for someone (or something). When I am unable to speak them out loud, I say them silently to myself. You can also write them over and over in a notebook or journal.

Consistent, persistent, and ceaseless repetition will uplift your conscious thinking, sink into your subconscious thought, and expand into the superconscious. What happens next is, without question, magic and money healing and manifestation. You will bring into your life more of what you want in a relaxed and pleasant way.

Here are a few of my favorites:

I am receiving; I am receiving now. I am receiving all the wealth that the Universe has for me now!

I love money and money loves me! It flows to me in avalanches of abundance! All of my needs, goals, and desires are now met instantaneously!

I have a substantial, reliable, constant financial income now. I receive money every day in miraculous ways!

Your money healing is a process you can put into action in an effortless, personal, and private way using the Magic Money Magnetizers above. What you've been doing has gotten you this far, and now you can mend your money wounds and expand into more abundance than ever. What are you waiting for?

---

**Holly Alexander is the author of the Magic Money Book Series: A Course in Creating Abundance. She's a serial entrepreneur, multiple business owner, philanthropist, wife, mom, avid traveler, reader, and explorer.**

**She believes you can have, do, and be everything you want to have, do, and be when you treat life and money with the respect they deserve. You can find out more at MagicMoneyBooks.com, and grab your free copy of _Beginning Magic Money_ at https://bit.ly/FreeBMM.**

# CHAPTER 6

# Voice Dialogue
## Talk to Your Pain

### BY REV. DR. STEPHANIE RED FEATHER

## My Story

I've been an empath my entire life, but for the first 30 years, I didn't know it. My ability to absorb others' energies, expectations, values, and beliefs defined the first three decades of my life, including my first career choice. As I grew into adulthood, the once creative intuitive child had to bury her sensitivities to "succeed in the real world." My spiritual awakening—and thus my healing journey—began stirring on the eve of the new millennium, 1999, and launched full force in 2002 when I separated from the Air Force after being an officer for ten years. Yes, you heard me right—an empath in the military.

I left the Air Force not because I knew what I wanted to do next, but because a quiet voice in my heart told me it was time to get out. After planning and saving for a career as a financial advisor—an investment of $25,000 and over 12 months of preparation—I quit in less than six months. I hated it. I had no idea how to be a compassionate boss to myself, and the flat-out honest truth was that I didn't know who I was or what I wanted.

A five-year period of time that I have since called the spiritual crucible ensued. In every way imaginable, I was being cooked down, stripped, purified, and alchemically transformed into a new substance. But I did not go willingly. I didn't understand the concept of shamanic death and rebirth, nor did I have the tools for managing such a monumental personal transfiguration. I cried, screamed, cussed at God, and wondered if I would ever find my way through. At the end of those five years, nothing in my life looked the same as when it started: city, state, house, job, marriage, car, possessions, financial status, everything was different.

Yet, my time in the crucible paved the way for the manifestation of my soul's purpose. When I emerged from that period of intense spiritual initiation, I felt a calling to help others through their own awakening experiences. I started my spiritual healing and coaching business as a result in 2007. Over the last 20+ years, I have done an immense amount of inner work, studied with multiple teachers, gained certification in numerous modalities, and taught others in similar fields. I have worked intimately with the divine feminine mysteries, shamanic consciousness, energy concepts, the shadow, and embodiment practices. And, of course, I learned to embrace that I was an empath and walk with my empathic gifts as an ally instead of a liability.

I have always been fascinated with the human psyche and one of the modalities that has given me great insight into my own inner workings is Voice Dialogue. While it is one of the more "secular" modalities I am trained in, it is way more than basic talk therapy and has transformed my inner landscape. I have a completely different relationship with my triggers and wounds and can be at choice in my emotional reactions. I am adept at determining "who" is talking and what part or parts of my psyche are needing attention, acknowledgement, or to be heard. Voice Dialogue is a practical tool that lends itself well to a self-help format, and I hope that this tool gives you access to immense healing, insight, and transformation.

## The Tool

### WHAT IS VOICE DIALOGUE?

Voice Dialogue is a technique where you can talk to any part of your psyche to find out its point of view and why it acts in your life the way it does. Your psyche is made up of a vast number of parts, and common examples include a protector, people pleaser, inner critic, taskmaster, and wounded child(ren). Each part has its own reason for being, purpose, perspective, and influence. Some of these parts are primary (the ones that are usually driving the bus) and are a major component of our personality. Other parts are unconscious or play a more minor role in our lives.

These parts are fascinating because they each act autonomously (occasionally pairing up with other parts when their purposes align) and are very myopic in their focus. Psyche parts are created in response to major wounding or traumatic events in our childhood, as well as formed around repeated messages and modeling we received from parents and other significant influences. Parts are always created for a specific purpose, such as to protect us, make sure we get our needs met, or ensure a painful experience never happens again. Difficulty often shows up, however, when a part continues to employ its strategies long after the need or threat has expired. Then it can act at cross-purposes with our current desires.

When this occurs, you might have repeated experiences of:

♦ An internal force that seems to sabotage every dream
♦ Being stuck in old patterns you can't seem to break
♦ Being unable to control your behavior when you get triggered, despite your best intentions
♦ An adversarial relationship with your ego
♦ Inner conflict that keeps you stuck

Our society is organized around the concepts of polarity—right and wrong, good and bad—which causes us to unwittingly put our internal voices at odds with one another. This creates incredible inner conflict and forces us to validate one opinion while invalidating the rest. With Voice Dialogue, you have the opportunity to recognize that *all* of your opinions (all the voices in your head) are valid! This doesn't mean you have to *act* on all of them, but in allowing each part to be heard and acknowledging them as legitimate, it diffuses the tension and ambiguity.

For example, if you are considering moving, you might be confused and stuck because one part (say The Adventurer) says, *yes, let's do it! I like new environments and challenges!* Your Security Advisor might be more cautious, saying, *well, let's think about this. Don't you think you need to have more money in savings first? Moving is expensive. And your car is getting old, too.* Then there might be a wounded child who is screaming because of the bad experience you had when your family moved at age seven, where you felt abandoned, lonely, and missed your friends.

None of these points of view are wrong. Every feeling and concern is valid. When you can sort out the source of each of the seemingly conflicting messages in your head, it will help you make a clearer decision. Think of yourself as the CEO of your company. You are sitting in the board room, taking input from each of your directors (relevant parts of your psyche). While you listen thoughtfully and consider each director's input, you are the one who makes the final decision. Each of your directors has their own priorities and concerns. But you are responsible for the health and well-being of the company (you!) as a whole.

Further, Voice Dialogue isn't limited just to conversations with parts of your psyche. If you can conceive of it, you can have a conversation with it! This includes body parts, diseases and conditions, angels and spirit guides, behaviors, beliefs, archetypes, and ideas. This tool allows you direct access not only to parts or conditions causing you pain but also access to the bigger picture, spiritual guidance, past lives, and inspiration.

## HOW TO PREPARE FOR A VOICE DIALOGUE SESSION

Make sure you conduct this conversation during a time when you'll be undisturbed. Set aside at least 30 minutes to an hour. I prefer to ground and center, light a candle, activate my altar, and call in my spiritual team when engaging in this kind of work. In whatever way feels right to you, take a few moments to create sacred space and prepare energetically, physically, emotionally, and spiritually.

Your conversation can be written out on paper or typed on a computer, so organize yourself based on your preference. Either way, it will resemble a script (below), and it is recommended that you label each exchange as such so you can keep track of who said what:

You:
Name of Part:
You:
Name of Part:

Choose the part, problem, or pain you want to talk to. Have a short, clear description so when you call it forward, your parts will be sure about who you are asking to come online. Examples might be, "I want to talk to the pain in my left hip." "I want to talk to the part of me that constantly berates my partner." "I want to talk to the part of me that always caves in to everyone else's wants." "I want to talk to the parts who have an opinion about my desire to move."

As the facilitator, it is important to keep a few key concepts in mind. First, the idea in talking to any part is not to pick a fight, make the part wrong, or kill it off. Being confrontational or combative only puts it on the defensive and will net little benefit. Second, be as curious, objective, and detached as possible, not getting sucked into how that part makes you feel, but staying neutral and listening dispassionately like you've never met this part before. Third, be honest. Parts are smart and can tell if you have an agenda, which might make them suspicious of you and keep them from being forthcoming, especially child parts. Fourth, it's okay to comment (as long as it is genuine and not patronizing) like, "I understand why you feel that way." "That would upset me, too." Or, "I hear you."

## CONDUCTING THE VOICE DIALOGUE SESSION

You (the aware ego or whole self) is the one conducting the interview. The part, problem, or pain is the interviewee. You will essentially be going back and forth, playing the role of both facilitator and facilitated. This may feel a bit awkward at first, but allow the conversation to flow and don't censure what you "hear." Trust what comes through you.

When you are ready to begin, make some kind of physical movement as a cue that you are now bringing that part online. Do not skip this. It is an important signal that creates separation from normal everyday activities and lets your psyche know the conversation is commencing. The movement can be simple such as standing up and sitting down, spinning around once in your chair, or clapping your hands twice. It is like a director saying, "Action!"

When you feel the part is present, double-check and ask, "Is this the part of me that always caves into everyone else's wants?" When you get an affirmative response, begin your conversation.

### What Questions to Ask

If you're dealing with a particularly emotional part, such as a child part, or a body pain, you might start by asking, "How do you feel?"

A good set of standard questions to ask includes:

- How old was I when you were created?
- What was going on in my life when you were created?
- What name do you want me to call you?
- What is your purpose in my life?
- How do you act in my life—or—what triggers you into action?
- What do you want me to know about you?

Get creative. Ask whatever questions make sense in the flow of your conversation. When you are complete with your dialogue, end by repeating the physical movement you used to start the session: stand up and sit down, spin the opposite direction in your chair, or clap your hands twice. This is like the director saying, "Cut!" and allows you to separate from the part and come back into your aware ego or everyday self. It may take a few minutes to make the transition, so shake any intense energy off your arms, smudge yourself, drink some water, or walk around for a bit to ensure you are completely back in your body and grounded in the present.

## FOLLOWING UP

Right after your session, reflect and journal on what you learned. This can help you connect dots and see patterns. Additionally, make notes about how you felt when you were in that part. Did you feel tense or relaxed? Scared or confident? Were you skeptical, angry, mistrusting? What physical symptoms registered in your body? These can give you important clues during regular daily life as to which part is "running the show" or has at least been triggered.

Depending on the issue you are dealing with, you could benefit from multiple conversations with that part. In addition, there are almost certainly a few other parts that are related or have a role to play as well, so conversations with them can give you a bigger picture perspective. In future dialogues, you can even ask, "What part would like to come forward and speak with me?" Just be sure to ask its name and purpose.

If you talk to a lot of parts, over time, you might want to create a simple spreadsheet that includes the date, name of the part, and a summary of the conversation.

## WHAT TO DO IF YOU NEED MORE SUPPORT

If being both the facilitator and the part is challenging or if you have difficulty switching back and forth between them, then hire a trained Voice Dialogue coach to facilitate you. On rare occasions, a part might be non-verbal, and sometimes a part is so emotionally overwhelming that you desire to have an experienced facilitator guiding you. You can consult my resources section below to schedule a session with me.

I also find that, while I *can* facilitate myself, there are times when I want to be able to drop deeply into the part to have a fuller experience of it and not have to manage both roles. When you are in the part for a continuous period of time (and not switching between facilitator and facilitated), it can help you identify subtle nuances as well as map out in your physical-energetic-emotional body exactly how that part feels. This can help you identify more easily when and how that part is acting in your life.

## RESOURCES

Go to my website www.BlueStarTemple.org/ug2sh2 to find a bonus list of questions you can ask during a Voice Dialogue session and a discount code for scheduling a one-hour Voice Dialogue session with me.

---

Rev. Dr. Stephanie Red Feather is a divine feminine change agent and champion of empaths. An award-winning author of the #1 international best-seller, *The Evolutionary Empath: A Practical Guide for Heart-Centered Consciousness*, her passion is to help fellow sensitive souls break out of energetic jail and become co-creators of new earth consciousness. As a shamanic minister, workshop facilitator, and prolific creator of spiritual tools, Stephanie has helped thousands to connect with their sacred self and heal their human wounds.

Stephanie is the founder and director of Blue Star Temple, an online resource for spiritual seekers to learn energetic skills, hone empathic abilities, access spiritual knowledge, and connect with cosmic consciousness. Her specialties include masculine-feminine balance, boundaries, energy hygiene, shadow work, shamanic consciousness, embodiment, and celestial mysteries. Above all, she honors her clients' and students' personal truth and experience while facilitating deeper initiation into their own inner mysteries.

Stephanie's life has been an unusual fusion of creativity, spirituality, and hard science, first attending a performing arts school in adolescence, then earning a degree in applied mathematics before becoming an Air Force officer. She holds a Master's and Doctorate in shamanic studies from Venus Rising University and has been a mesa carrier in the Pachakuti Mesa Tradition of Peru since 2005. Her uncommon talent of bridging left- and right-brain worlds amplifies her ability to make esoteric concepts accessible and practical.

Stephanie is also a contributing author to the #1 best-seller *Chaos to Clarity*. When she isn't writing or facilitating workshops, you can find Stephanie engaging her wilder feminine creative energy through making jewelry and medicine pieces, getting her hands dirty in the garden, riding horses, and nerding out over science documentaries.

You can find her books, courses, meditations, and workshops at BlueStarTemple.org and her resource page designed for readers of this book at BlueStarTemple.org/ug2sh2.

# CHAPTER 7

# Breathwork
## Deep Relaxation Through Conscious Breath

### BY NEELAM SINGH, E-RYT, CHHC

## The Story

The leaves had begun to change in color, in preparation for the winter months ahead. It was a crisp, beautiful day, perfect for a long walk in the woods. Instead, here I was waiting patiently on the examination table for my doctor to arrive. I didn't mind the wait. The doctor, aside from being my primary care physician, was also a very attentive listener. Today, I was hoping the blood work results would shed some light on my fatigue, brain fog, and sudden teary episodes, which had become frequent lately.

After the physical checkup, the doctor paused and looked up from her laptop. "Neelam," she sounded somber. "Since your last physical, your A1C level has jumped from 5.3% (*healthy*) to 5.7% (*pre-diabetic*). Your Vitamin D levels are low, and this can influence moods. Your estrogen levels are still high, which is good; however, your hormone panel indicates you are potentially in early meno-pause. Do you still menstruate regularly?" she asked.

I was astounded and trying to process what I had just heard. Series of thoughts were already whirling through my mind. *How could this be possible? Pre-diabetic? Menopausal, already?* There was no family history of diabetes. Based on genetics, I wasn't expecting menopause to begin for another seven years.

"My periods have been regular," I responded feebly. The doctor replied, "Neelam, you have been leading a healthy lifestyle. Normally, losing as little as 5-10% of total bodyweight brings down the A1C numbers. However, that is not an option for you as your weight is already in the healthy range. Make sure you work outside the house during the morning hours. That, along with Vitamin D, should help."

I left the doctor's office in disbelief, trying to make sense out of it all. My family and friends often joked about my healthy lifestyle, which had naturally weaved into my life since 2005. *I led a healthy lifestyle, practiced yoga, and was soon to finish my yoga teacher training. What more could I have done?*

For the next couple of days, I took a step back from the everyday grind. I parked myself on the bedroom couch, trying to acknowledge the emotional storm, giving myself space to reflect. I decided to take a long, hard look at my life as an observer, shutting out all the outside chatter.

What I saw initially overwhelmed me. A continuous chasing and checking off a never-ending list of responsibilities had left me drained. Unease and mind chatter in the background had been there all along. Long hours of reflection and analysis of life since 2005 followed. About two weeks before Christmas that year, I recalled repeatedly listening to my doctor's voicemail, "We received your blood test results. The cause of the long-suffering painful symptoms is chronic Lyme. It means you likely have arthritis now . . ." Surprisingly, I felt a sense of relief wash over me. For the first time in seven years, there was proof that my pain was real. I was hopeful that after the rounds of antibiotics prescribed by the primary care physician, my knee pain would heal. Well, it didn't.

I began to doubt my recovery when the specialist said, "You are lucky; it's only arthritis, and it hasn't yet affected you neurologically." And now, after months of treatment, there was still no relief from the pain. Summer was around the corner, the pool and beaches were calling. My daughter had just turned five, and my son was fifteen months old. The next level of treatment required me to self administer intravenous (IV) antibiotics.

At that point, I decided to take charge of healing the pain. I committed and affirmed to myself, *thus declaring it to the Universe*, "I'm ready to heal and live a pain-free life. My children deserve a happy and healthy mom." With continuous efforts and a series of synchronicities, by Fall 2006, I was finally able to heal the pain. It was short of a miracle. For the first time, I experienced an organized mind's power and how it can positively influence the body's healing.

Till now, my experiences in life had directly influenced my moods, emotions, and thoughts, and vice versa. Always trying to control outside situations to fix my inner experience left me exhausted. I remember growing up watching my dad worry a lot! I thought it was a normal part of life. On the contrary, I remember my mom grounded and carefree. So the seeds of worry and calm were both sown in my childhood. In my world, worrying was synonymous with caring. Growing up, I unconsciously nurtured the worry-seed. Now, its hold has grown past the mind, affecting my body.

As I continued going down memory lane, I recalled how my quest to find inner wellbeing began through books. Dr. Brian Weiss's books introduced me to life beyond life, and his visually guided meditations at Omega Institute, kindled my curiosity to explore the energy body. Thus over the next few years, I ended up training as a Reiki Master Teacher and Integrated Energy Therapy Master-Instructor. Eckhart Tolle's teachings inspired me to practice living fully in the here and now.

At the end of reflecting on the past many years, I now began to see vast, rich experiences of healing, exploration, connection to the inner self, resilience, and perseverance. *If I had managed to heal my pain in 2006, what was stopping me now?* I was motivated enough to get off the couch and take charge of my mindset and vitality once again.

For the first time, I consciously tried to slow the pace of life, pausing to listen to my body, and understand what the symptoms were trying to reveal. I would close my eyes and take slow deep breaths, with long extended exhales. I began to notice this slow, quiet practice calming the overactive brain, increasing productivity, and energizing the body for the rest of the day. After three months, I successfully finished my 200 hour Yoga Teacher Training and began to teach yoga.

As my breath-practice became consistent, the quality and texture of the breath became more evident. Breath is very much a reflection of the mind's state. Some days the breath flowed with extreme ease. It was soft, fluid, expansive, and deep. On other days it was shallow, choppy, and constricted. Breathing intentionally and deliberately helped me bring my awareness into my body. Over time, this practice improved my relationship with my feelings. Slowly, I began to acknowledge and accept them as they showed up. I would start by placing a hand on my heart, breathing, and letting the emotions flow as I stayed present to all the sensations in my body. I began to look forward to connecting with my inner self.

During the Integrative Nutrition Health Coaching Certification and Functional Nutrition Programs, I learned how gut and brain health were closely connected. It was not enough to nourish just the body with a well-balanced, nutrient-dense diet. It was equally critical to prevent stress, improve sleep quality, and fuel the mind with healthy thoughts, practices like meditation. The gut-brain connection has provided immense insights for myself and my clients. Physical, mental, emotional, and spiritual health are the cornerstones of sustainable holistic wellbeing. So when a friend invited me to join her for the Inner Engineering Program with Sadhguru in Chicago, I instantly agreed. This program changed my perception of life forever and paved my way to participate later in Shoonya and then Samayama both advanced meditation programs offered by Isha Foundation.

Chronic stress can put health at risk. The brain doesn't distinguish between a real danger or a perceived one. During chronic stress, the body responds by activating the sympathetic nervous system (SNS), the fight-or-flight response. This response overrides the parasympathetic nervous system (PNS), the rest and relaxation response of the body. This results in digestive distress, low absorption of nutrients, elevated blood sugar, and weight gain may occur. During the relaxation response, the heart rate and blood pressure decrease, digestion improves, the liver stores sugar, immune response improves, muscles relax, and cellular regeneration is activated. The two systems—SNS and PNS function in a complementary manner; when one is on, the other is off.

For the body to achieve homeostasis (physiological balance), the more time one spends in the rest and digest mode, the better. Taking a few conscious breaths is a simple way to connect with your innate healing power. First, become aware of your breath, taking slow, smooth breaths in, and long extended breaths out. Simple slow, deep breathing with emphasis on long exhalation can promote the body's relaxation response (PNS). With consistent and dedicated practice, it becomes effortless to carry this practice off our seat into our real-life. One can breathe with awareness doing daily chores, washing dishes, walking, talking, listening, and even while waiting in traffic.

Your breath is your companion from the day you take your first breath until the last. To realize its full potential, all you have to do is be aware of its presence at any given time. It can carry you through the highs and lows of life.

Conscious breath practice stimulates the right side of the brain, which quietens the thoughts. It's like taking your right side of the brain to the gym, more like strengthening your brain muscles. If you have trouble sitting for practice, try going for a walk, jog, stretch, practice yoga, or find any movement appropriate for your body. If your mind is anxious, try journaling first. Write on a piece of paper, then shred or burn it. You now may find yourself better prepared for a breath meditation practice.

## The Tool

Now let's walk you through a deep relaxation session. The full session includes three phases, and they appear as headings when you read through. Your experience is best when guided by another. A recorded version of this practice is available online on my website for a free download.

Click link: https://www.momentinspired.com/resources

Find a quiet space. You may choose to play soothing music. Make sure your seat is just comfortable enough to sit and practice and not doze off. You may choose to sit on a chair or a couch with straight back support and rest your feet on the ground. If sitting on the floor, sit in easy pose, crossing legs in front of you. You may use the wall support and keep your legs long as an alternative. If you practice lying down on your back, make sure you place a rolled blanket under your knees to support your back.

## LET'S BEGIN THE PRACTICE OF CONSCIOUS BREATHING

- ◆ Settle in your comfortable seat. Close your eyes or keep looking down on the floor if you rather keep them open.
- ◆ You may keep your hands on your thighs facing up and the elbows close to the sides of your body.
- ◆ Sit nice and tall and yet relaxed.
- ◆ Become aware of your shoulders and slide them back and down towards your hips.
- ◆ Chin parallel to the floor and head in the center of your shoulders.
- ◆ Become aware of your seat and feel the support underneath your sitting bones.
- ◆ Begin to notice the temperature around you as it touches your bare skin. How does it feel?... Cool?... Warm?... Muggy?
- ◆ Notice the sounds around you, and pay attention to your ears listening.
- ◆ If you happen to be outdoors, pay attention to the natural sounds.
- ◆ Now turn your attention inwards. Where do you feel your breath? In your chest or belly or both? Just notice.
- ◆ Sometimes, it's helpful to place one hand on your heart

and the other on your belly when you start breathing.
- Bring your attention to your heart center. What do you notice? How do you feel now? Notice the sensation. There is no right or wrong. It just is.
- Do you notice the taste in your mouth?
- Now bring your attention to the thoughts arising.

## NOW LET'S ADD AWARENESS OF THE BREATH

- Notice your breath. Feel it in your belly, notice the hand rise as you breathe in, and the ribs expand sideways.
- Notice the hand sink as you breathe out.
- As you take a full breath in through the nose, notice the belly rise, and your chest's inner walls expand sideways.
- Take a slow, long breath out as you exhale through partially parted lips and notice the relaxation that follows.
- With the next breath in, notice the lifting feeling within and breathe until you feel as if the breath has reached your chin.
- Now with your next breath out slowly release the air out of your lungs through your partially parted lips. Notice the belly sink in, and the belly button press back towards the spine.
- Take a breath in and notice the expansion in your upper body.
- Take a breath out and notice the inner walls of your torso soften as they sink in.
- Continue breathing in fully and breathing out deeply. If possible, try to breathe in and breathe out through your nostrils, moving forward.

## YOU'LL NOW BE GUIDED THROUGH A BODY SCAN

- Bring your awareness to each body part when mentioned. If you are unable to feel a body part, it's ok. Move to the next one and focus on it.
- Take a breath in and feel both feet. Focus on feet, and as you take a breath out, let them relax. With your next breath, move your awareness to your ankles.

- Now feel your lower legs and let them soften.
- With your next full breath, begin to focus on your knees.
- As you take an extended breath out, let your breath flow to your knees. Let your awareness travel up to your thighs.
- Take a full breath in and a breath out. Let both legs relax.
- Continue breathing in fully and breathing out deeply as you continue scanning your body parts.
- Notice your hips, now move your attention to your belly.
- Your awareness travels up to your ribs as you inhale and exhale.
- Focus on the heart center and chest and notice the chest expanding and contracting as you breathe.
- Bring your attention to your hands and then arms.
- Now notice your shoulders and let them relax and release down.
- Become aware of your neck and head. Soften the face and relax the jaw.
- Feel the breath in your chest, shoulders, arms, neck, face, and head and breathe out, releasing any stored tension in these parts.
- If you notice your mind wander, gently bring it back to the ebb and flow of your breath.
- Take a full slow breath in and an extended long breath out. Stay here as long as you like and just notice and focus on your breath sensation. Try to observe the thoughts that may surface. Let them come and go. Continue breathing consciously. Full, deep breaths in and long extended breaths out . . . Stay with your breath . . . Pay attention to the ebb and flow of your breath.
- When you are ready to come out, take a deep breath in and a breath out. Feel your body and feel yourself rooting into the earth through your feet or your sit bones. Notice how you feel. Then bring the palms of your hands together.
- Now rub them together until you feel some warmth in your palms. Place your palms on your closed eyes for some time.

- Gently release your hands to your thighs and slowly open your eyes and enjoy the pause.
- Notice how you feel now. Has anything shifted in your experience?

## SIMPLE STEPS FOR DEEPENING YOUR BREATH PRACTICE:

- Place one hand on your belly.
- Take a deep, slow, smooth breath in and inflate your abdomen like a balloon and feel your hand rising as it rests on your belly.
- Notice chest rise and the ribs expand sideways.
- Take a deep long extended breath out and allow your belly to relax.
- Repeat for 5-10 breaths or as needed.

Life situations haven't changed, and neither has the content of my life. What has changed is the context. Every moment is a choice to either react or respond to life. The conscious breath practice has helped my clients, and I break many cycles of fight or flight responses. It has prevented chronic stress burnout, allowing to experience relaxation in the body, far beyond the yoga mat.

"If you look at life on the surface,
it is brutal. If you look at it with some sensitivity,
it is beautiful. But if you look at it with great depth,
everything here is magical."
—Sadhguru

Tune out the noise and tune in within. For a change to occur, constant motion isn't needed. Sit still, connect to the innate intelligence within, and listen. Incredible strength lies within us quietly in the stillness. It's waiting to be recognized. It's a journey that ignites the human spirit and nurtures the seeds of hope, peace, and joy! Once you anchor in the current moment with your breath and body, you can choose to respond to life with the newfound awareness. It's where the potential for empowered life begins.

I invite you to join the free private Facebook group by clicking on the link below: https://www.facebook.com/groups/ReadyIam/

Click on the link for the deep relaxation session recording and other free offerings below:
https://www.momentinspired.com/resources

Website link: https://www.momentinspired.com

Facebook Business Page: https://www.facebook.com/MomentInspired/

---

Neelam Singh, E-RYT, CHHC, founded momentinspired.com, first as a digital scrapbook for recording and sharing her journey of living in the present moment. In 2015 it morphed into an online Health and Wellness business platform to support her clients globally. Neelam guides & navigate their journeys to optimal and holistic wellbeing through sustainable lifestyle practices.

Neelam is invited to speak at health events and teaches yoga. She offers private and groups online yoga and nutrition programs.

Neelam is a Certified Integrative Nutrition Health Coach, who focuses on Hormone, Gut Health and Stress prevention. She also studied Functional Nutrition. Neelam is a Certified Vinyasa, Yin Yoga, Yoga Nidra, and a Children's Yoga Teacher. She trained as a Reiki Master/Teacher and Integrated Energy Therapy Master-Instructor.

Neelam Singh is a Computers & Information Systems graduate from the University of Maryland. She worked in the Software field for several years.

She loves to walk, travel, read, and explore. She lives with her family in the suburbs of Virginia, right outside of Washington, D.C.

# CHAPTER 8

# Spiritual Grounding
## Moving from Ruin to Radiance

### BY DAWNE HORIZONS, HHC, LMT

## My Story

I can honestly say I don't look like what I've been through! The Spiritual Grounding tool I'm about to share with you is what I used to get me through sexual trauma, emotional abuse, neglect, abandonment, an adulterous marriage, suicidal thoughts, and raising five children from newborn to age 14 as a divorced, single mom. This tool literally saved my life and helped me move from Ruin to Radiance in my personal life, as a mother, and in my business, and it can be a catalyst for you too. I am not only surviving but thriving as a result of doing the much-needed soul and spiritual work to release the trauma I had experienced. Let me tell you how it all happened.

I was so busy being a wife and mother taking care of my five children and the house that I lost myself. I did not take time for me. There was no time for me. I found approval in doing so I just kept doing to make myself feel approved of those I was serving. One day I was in the basement doing laundry, a never-ending task with five kids, and a bedwetter! I heard a door upstairs close; I knew my husband had come home, but I jumped! I noticed myself standing there in the laundry room afraid with my heart racing, so I asked myself, why did you jump and act as if you were abused? It was then that I realized I was abused!

At that moment, I heard a heavenly voice say, "You married your father." Stunned, I said, "Oh my God! I did!" I saw my last 18 years with this man so clearly in that moment that I could not argue with the voice I distinctively heard or my instant and very rude awakening. I was in shock and, at the same time, definite agreement. You see, my father was selfish, self-centered, materialistic, charismatic, and a showman. He pretended or at least he thought in his own mind he was a great father because he provided for me, but that's all he did. He bought clothes, food, and made sure I went to school, but he offered nothing in the area of love, affection, affirmation, or quality time. And every promise he ever made to me he never kept, no matter that I got good grades, behaved in school and all the other hoops he had me jump through. And right then I realized my husband was the same type of man and that I had been abused, neglected and traumatized by my father, my maternal grandfather and my husband. All three men in my life were the same and treated me the same. Although they loved me, they had a funky way of showing it. I experienced great pain and freedom all at the same time because what was hidden, although painful, was revealed.

I've had several epiphanies in my life, but this was one that woke me up and altered the course of my life. I realized my low self-esteem, low self-confidence, shyness, need for approval, and pleasing people by performing or doing for them. I realized I was always helping others and taking care of others, but no one was taking care of me, and neither was I. My self-healing journey and discovery began. My children had to heal too, and they weren't as aware or open to the opportunity as I was, so there was a period of time that they were fighting and acting up in school. They didn't know how to process the breakup of our family and once seemingly happy home. A couple of times, I had to call the police and get help with my eldest son because he had seen his father be abusive to me, so he tried to follow suit and was abusive to my eldest daughter and me. This was devastating, and I had to be strong for myself and my children since I didn't have any family support. His family shunned me as if I was the one doing wrong, and they didn't believe the adultery even with pictures, passport and receipts I showed them. They tried to make me feel like I was crazy, and they even took his side! I was at my lowest. Since he was the breadwinner and I was a stay at home mom and homeschooling my children, I had no money for food or anything. I had to go to food pantries, and I had to fight the system just to get food stamps. I've heard it said that when you're on your back, you can only look up, and that's what I did. That's when I discovered my spiritual grounding, and it literally saved my life and brought me out of depression and despair. In time, it brought me from Ruin to Radiance.

Spiritual grounding is the tool I used to keep me from the darkest depression, suicide, and allowing others to continue to abuse me or living in bitterness and lack of forgiveness. After the long drawn out divorce, I discovered who I truly was and began to own my greatness and be authentically me. I found it ironic that you do not realize how bound you are until you are free, and I had found a freedom that I never knew my whole life!

In trying to restart my life after divorce and trying to rebuild from emotional and financial ruin, I again heard a voice. This time the voice gave me a very specific directive via the Holy Bible, Genesis 12:1 NIV: "Go from your country, your people, and your father's household to the land I will show you." Being born and raised in New York my whole life, 40 years at the time, this directive was shocking and scary! How was I, who had no money and knew no one out of state going to move and relocate with my five children? From there, another court battle ensued, and another self-healing journey began because I had to move from New York to Virginia, where I was directed. Thankfully, the judge saw through his lies and attempts to stop me, and she agreed that it was better for me to relocate with the children to provide a better life for them. Little did I know that this was a major set up for a comeback that I could not have dreamed of, and God used it to set me and my children in a position of healing, self-discovery, love, influence, faith, growth, freedom and prosperity.

## The Tool

Spiritual Grounding Steps:

1. Set your atmosphere playing soft inspirational background music.
2. Sit or lay down comfortably quieting your mind.
3. Set your intentions (i.e., release hurt, pain, past, forgiveness, etc...).
4. Pray, seeking spiritual guidance (speak and listen).
5. Engage deep breathing: in thru the diaphragm and slowly out through the mouth.
6. Use three drops essential oils (my preferred brand is Young Living) in your hand, rub three times clockwise to increase the frequency of the oil, then breathe in deeply. Next, apply the residue in your hands to your feet or wherever your intuition directs you. (Find more info about the oils at https://www.myyl.com/dawnehorizons)
7. As thoughts come to the surface of your mind, look at them, consider them, and get to the root, keep looking until you see a clear picture or memory of the past.
8. Recognize how you are feeling in your body and emotions as thoughts arise.
9. Allow the negative feelings to pass visualizing them coming out of you and away from you.
10. Recognize who you are and who you were created to be (you are not what happened to you, you are not what someone has done to you or you have done to someone. You are valuable and worthy no matter how, what, or when things happened in your life). Note: if you have trouble recognizing your true self, then more work is needed, and a private session would be helpful.
11. Deal with whatever feelings come up by releasing them, allowing peace, love, and forgiveness to flow in you and through you. Here is my mantra: (repeat this to yourself and out loud) "I release and let go of all that no longer serves me

in a positive and productive manner. I choose to let go. I forgive myself and those who hurt, used or abused me in any way. Hurt people hurt people, so I release ____ (enter the name of person, act, or event) I pray they too receive healing. I declare I am free! I am renewed! I am healed! I am whole!"
12. Now, Get up! Take this new attitude, healing, and empowerment to go about your day and your life expecting new, better experiences. Enjoy each day, be thankful for everything, everyone, and every experience. Live life to the full!

In closing, I want you to know that you can utilize these steps at any time and in any place, you need to process your pain. There were times I had to use them in the car driving or while craziness was happening around me. Once you know how to find your center, speak positive to yourself and allow negative feelings to flow away from you, you will realize how empowering this exercise is and use the steps you need at any given moment you need to be healed and free. Steps 10-12 can definitely be used 'on the go.' Allow these 12 steps to help you and heal you as you journey from Ruin to Radiance.

---

Dawne Horizons is an award-winning International Speaker and Healer. As a Certified Holistic Health Coach and Licensed Massage Therapist, she opened Dawne Horizons Spa & Wellness Center in 2006.

Dawne's purpose is to teach people how to Live Healthy Naturally: Spirit, Soul & Body with God's Medicine, essentially discipling them to live their "Best, Blessed Life Now," both inside and out! Dawne brings Education, Enlightenment & Empowerment to women looking for real answers about their health, spirituality, identity, and purpose. She has spoken to women all over the United States, Mexico, Guyana, and Grand Cayman Islands. She emphasizes getting to the Root cause of what ails you and not just treating the Fruit, helping women discover, uncover, and recover from trauma and abuse and the harmful effects they have on the body.

Dawne expanded her vision by working with the Senior Citizen Community in 2015, showing them love while relieving aches & pains with her "Senior Spa Day." In 2018 she expanded her Senior outreach to include Senior Movie Day, which is a combined Movie and Spa Day provided free to the community.

Dawne is that tangible person that can Coach, Correct, and Cheerlead you to Wellness & Wholeness. With almost 20 years of training and experience in Aromatherapy, Body Work and Massage, Dawne really knows how to help you heal from the inside out.

Dawne is a mother of three adult children and two teenage girls. She is a proud grandmother of two granddaughters. Lastly, Dawne is the primary caregiver to her mother with early onset Dementia for the past seven years. Caring for others truly is her motto and mission. Join Wellness Wisdom Wednesday with Dawne Horizons Live on Facebook & Instagram 9 pm weekly.

Dawne is Making Healthy Disciples.

Connect with Dawne @dawnehorizons on Facebook, Instagram, LinkedIn & Twitter

Follow #askdawne #makinghealthydisciples #wellnesswisdom #physicianhealthyself #speaklife and #dawnehorizons to stay abreast of tools and strategies to heal yourself and live free daily.

# CHAPTER 9

# Flat Abs
## Physics, and the Jedi
### BY DR. KIM BYRD-RIDER, MPT, DPT, MPSYCH

## My Story

I was 60 pounds too fat after having two children in my 20s (mid-1990s). But oh, how I enjoyed putting that weight on! I inhaled ice cream and potato chips with sour cream dip as my pregnancy muumuu dress got bigger and bigger. What a delight!

So, like we are all told, I went to the gym, worked out, and did 300 sit-ups with a weight on my chest, because that is what people did back then to lose weight and flatten their belly. After earning a master's and a doctorate in physical therapy, I now know an easier, more effective, and safer way to get flat abs, even after childbirth. By the way, going to college was a very expensive way to learn how to flatten abs. I don't recommend it.

I hated going to the gym so much that I decided to teach the step aerobics class, so I was forced to show up! Remember step aerobics? It is dead now.

Just as step aerobics began its slow death, yoga was being born and delivered into the mainstream. Madonna started doing yoga; she was the pivotal instigator. Her body slimmed down, and she went from a chubby "Material Girl" to looking like a thoroughbred horse. Oprah asked Madonna on her national TV show, "What is up with your new body?" She said, "All I do is yoga. A man from India lives in my house and teaches me every day."

You can imagine that everyone in Oklahoma City, Oklahoma, called our gym to ask, "Do you have a yoga class?" My opportunist fitness manager answered, "Of course we do. It is on Mondays at 6:00. Come in now and sign up with our gym." We did not have a yoga class, nor did anyone else in town. At that time in all of America, only hippies from the 1960s knew what yoga was, and meditation was non-existent. All our gym really had was an empty slot on Mondays at 6:00.

An emergency aerobic teachers' meeting took place on the Thursday before the fictitious Monday yoga class. My manager asked us, "Who wants to teach the yoga class on Monday?" No one even knew what yoga was. We looked back and forth at each other, "What's yoga? Do you mean yogurt?"

Well, I worshiped Madonna. She was my idol. I was the "Material Girl" in high school during the 1980s! I wore the crop tops, all the bangles, and even had the highlighted permed messy hair. When I heard her say on Oprah that she did yoga, I immediately found the only yoga class operating in a small city nearby and went the next day to check it out. It was revolutionary. I came out feeling better than when I went in. That was unheard of in aerobics. After aerobics, you feel road hard and put away wet!

I whispered very quietly to a co-teacher in the back of that Thursday meeting so no one could hear, "I tried it. I was higher than a kite afterward." It was probably because I was running my mouth, but the manager turns to me, hands me a brochure, and says, "You're it! Now go get trained in this workshop over the weekend, and you start on Monday." *Wow! Okay.* The first thing my new yoga teacher at the workshop said to me on Saturday morning was, "One weekend does not a yoga teacher make." Then, I got scared.

I started teaching yoga that Monday. I also started a two-year teacher training program and discovered a new way to view life. Because of the high demand and a lack of yoga teachers in the

1990s, all the fitness centers wanted me two-three days a week, and I taught at 11 different fitness centers, military bases, and independent living centers. I taught 25 yoga classes per week for seven years. I loved it, but I wasn't sure if I was hurting people. I asked myself, *What profession does this for a living? Oh, physical therapists.*

So, I went to physical therapy school for the next eight years and kept teaching yoga! I even taught yoga to my fellow students in the basement of the University of Oklahoma. As a clinical physical therapist, I realized there was a huge psychological role of pain going unaddressed in my patients. Back to school I went for a psychology degree while working in hospitals to complete the lenses I look through to treat patient pain. That's how I became a physical therapist, a psychologist, a professor, a meditator, and a yoga teacher.

I did it because I was too fat. Who said being fat was bad for you? Now, let's move on to the right way to flatten your abs...you will not be doing 300 sit-ups with a weight, lucky you!

For easier learning watch a video about the following tool:

## The Tool

### FLAT ABS

How would you feel if your abs were flat, they stayed flat, and all you had to do was an easy little breathing technique? How would your life change if your back pain went away? What if your pelvic floor were stronger, sex was better, and urine leaks went away?

Besides flattening your abs, the unique additional benefits of this breathing technique include:

◆ Lung muscle strengthening: automatic diaphragm and intercostal muscles exercise
◆ Pelvic floor strengthening: automatic Kegel exercises
◆ Spine stabilizing and strengthening: automatic spinal multifidi muscle exercise

As a physical therapist, I can tell you all these benefits are easily achievable, and almost everyone is going about training their abs wrong. How do I know? Most people are doing sit-ups (or sit-up type exercises) to flatten their abs. Sit-ups mainly train the six-pack (rectus abdominis muscle), which is a superficial narrow strip down the front of the trunk that produces forward bending, a sit-up motion. A different muscle needs to be strengthened to flatten the abs and pull in the "love handles" above the hips. Sit-up exercises are not focusing on that muscle. That muscle is the deep transverse abdominis (TvA).

The TvA muscle wraps around the entire trunk and looks just like a woman's corset from the 1800s. Like a corset, the TvA muscle runs from the ribs to the pelvis and all the way around the trunk. The TvA muscle laces itself into the spine via a strong leathery material called the thoraco-lumbar fascia. It laces itself into the front strip of the trunk with a similar leathery material called the linea alba. Doesn't that sound amazing? We have a muscle that acts like a corset and laces up the front and up the back with leather!

That muscle is a winner for flattening the abs and making our waistline smaller. By the way, that is exactly what the corset of the 1800s was created to do; shrink and flatten the waistline all the way around the trunk. Now, how do we strengthen the corset muscle, the TvA?

It is easy. We figure out what action the muscle performs, and then we do that action with an extra load for additional strengthening. Transverse means side-to-side or across. The transverse abdominis (TvA) muscle fibers run side to side or horizontally. The TvA action of the TvA is for the waistline to get smaller. How do we use conscious effort to take our waistline from wide to small? And how do we load that?

It is simple. We take a look at the TvA muscle's jobs and then replicate those jobs with a load. We did the same thing with the six-pack (rectus abdominis muscle) decades ago. The six-pack curls the spine forward, so we do a sit-up motion to train it. That forward spinal bend puts a lot of stress on the low back. Then, we add a weight on the chest to increase the intensity of the exercise, thus increasing the detrimental load to the low back, exponentially. The repeated sit-up motion or forward spine bend causes damage to the low back discs. Voila, you have back pain or sciatica you can't get rid of. On a brighter note, the TvA has two jobs:

1.  The TvA muscle stabilizes the spine during activities, holding the two halves of the body together; the upper body and the lower body. More spine stabilizing power in the trunk during activities and sports is a fantastic benefit to strengthening the TvA. The back becomes more stable and less painful as the TvA gets stronger, but how do we use that as an exercise? We can't really.

2.  The TvA muscle is also a forced exhaler. The TvA contracts or gets stronger when we do forced exhale breathing like coughing or sneezing. Okay, that we can replicate, but we can't add a weight to it. To replace the weight concept, we must intensify the forced exhale. In other words, we are increasing the muscle load by increasing the intensity of the forced exhale. We can't actually use the cough or sneeze because many times those actions also cause a detrimental downward force on the pelvic floor called a Valsalva maneuver. We need an inward and upward force to avoid the increased pressure complications associated with the Valsalva maneuver.

3.  The solution is a yoga breathing technique called Kapalabhati breathing. Other types of yogic forced breathing include the Breath of Fire and Ujjayi Breathing. Kapalabhati breathing focuses on the exhale resulting in a longer exhale, while Breath of Fire focuses on equal length of exhale and inhale. They are very similar. A gentler version of strengthening the TvA is performed during Ujjayi breathing, which is cued in many types of yoga classes. I would

advise using the Ujjayi breath during yoga class because it also strengthens the TvA. We will focus on Kapalabhati breathing because it has the most amount of intensity, like adding a weight to a sit-up.

To view a video version of this exercise, follow this link: https://www.byrdriderrehab.com/the-vibe-store/ ultimate-guide-to-self-healing/

## Kapalabhati Breathing

Sit tall with your back unsupported or you can lie down. Your body does not move. Your shoulders stay very still throughout the exercise. Only the belly moves as it goes in and out.

STEP 1
INHALE: BELLY EXPANDS AND GETS BIG.

STEP 2
EXHALE WITH A SUPER STRONG 'SHHHHHHH" SOUND, LIKE YOU ARE TELLING SOMEONE TO BE QUIET IN A LIBRARY HARSHLY AS IF YOU HAVE ALREADY TOLD THEM TO BE QUIET 10 TIMES. THE BELLY PULLS IN AND UP AS IT FLATTENS AND THE SIDE WALLS OF THE TRUNK PULL INWARD. NOTH-ING ELSE MOVES.

REPEAT STEPS 1 & 2 QUICKLY

For easier learning view this video: https://www.byrdriderrehab. com/the-vibe-store/ultimate-guide-to-self-healing/

Tip: The amount of load on the muscle is equal to the intensity of the "SHHHH" sound, so blow hard. Focus on the exhale, the inhale happens on its own. Continue until you don't want to do it anymore or get dizzy, about 2-3 sets of 25 times. You can also do this through your nose instead of your mouth if you want to clean out your nasal sinuses! Abdominals strengthen best when they are exercised/strengthened in this manner every day. Weights are not and cannot be used in this exercise. Weight training requires a 48-hour waiting period between exercise sessions. Kapalabhati breathing, the abdominal exercise here, does not require any waiting time between strengthening sessions.

## The Physics Voice

Kapalabhati Breathing is a forced exhale breathing technique performed via the mouth or nose for abdominal, diaphragm, pelvic floor, multifidus, and intercostal muscle strengthening/stretching (Deshmukh, & Bedekar, 2017). A person may sit or lie in supine but should not stand (due to decreased back support) during this breathing exercise. When exhaling, the transverse abdominis contracts maximally, and the waistline becomes smaller from posterior (back) to anterior (front) as a result. An added benefit is the strengthening of the spinal multifidi muscles and the pelvic floor muscles as they are automatically triggered to contract with the transverse abdominis by the nervous system (Ferla, Darski, Paiva, Sbruzzi, & Vieira, 2016; Yang, Lin, Chen, & Wang, 2016).

This exercise also trains an optimal exhale breathing pattern in conjunction with the transverse abdominis contraction, maintaining optimal intra-abdominal pressure during activities of daily living. Intra-abdominal pressure regulation is imperative in hernia, bladder prolapse, and uterus prolapse prevention (Qandeel, & O'Dwyer, 2016; Shek, & Dietz, 2016). Improved cardiovascular parameters and pulmonary parameters are benefits of this exercise (Jain, 2016). Residual air, always present in the bottom of the lungs to prevent collapse, is replaced with fresh air. Many times, sputum (phlegm) is expelled (spit out) during a Kapalabhati practice, or it leads to a productive cough. A productive cough expels sputum to clear the lungs, which is beneficial. Kapalabhati breathing is also one of the few abdominal exercises that can be performed in sitting.

## The Voice of the Jedi

It's foundational: The concept of focusing on the breath. The effect of directing your intellectual attention on the breath is the foundation for the expanded experience of you. That is what all great seekers have always known. There are various portals created with the different breath work experiences. So, you are encouraged to explore what is available to you and the many different ways to achieve a higher state of consciousness.

Each and every day, find your breath. Focus on it bringing in life. Keep it calm. Keep it in balance, and don't try to manipulate it. The ultimate experience here is one of self-observation. The use of mantras is effective in an overextended mind. The use of guided imagery begins to assist the human being in learning how to entrain new patterns of thinking. You are encouraged to explore all various means of working with the breath and the effects of different forms of meditation on your ability to be calm, to be at peace, to be centered, and to be fruitful in your creative inspirations. Each breath is filled with the life of all energy. All souls encompass all life. The mind cannot conceive of this, but it is all in the breath. The deeper you go in your exploration of your breath, the closer you become to the One.

There is a concept in the energy on this level of perception. It is the matter of the mind. It is the matter of the intellectual patterns of the thoughts that keep the people held hostage in their mind.

Here is a simple image to give you of the physical body and the logical mind, both here to support the inspiration of the soul. When the soul is inspired to get up and walk, the body responds. It does not run around 24/7 on its own, yet the mind does. Now, imagine if the mind lay in wait for the inspiration of the soul. Imagine if you were to train your mind to think intellectually only in support of an intuitive inspiration that surfaces. What if that is our truth?

What if, just like the body, the mind is here to support the soul's journey, but we have given it the power to define the journey? And what if your ability to quiet your mind allows you to experience your true divine self?

If this were your truth, how many minutes of each day would you choose thought over breath? Over inspirational integration of higher awareness? The breath is the connection to all life. Yet, the ego believes that thought is its connection to being.

The mind has identified its self with what it thinks, which can be removed from existence instantaneously according to the whim of the soul. Clear your field of all thought. Be open to explore the divine you; the you not limited by logic. See that. Each breath you are clearing your mind and creating the space to explore your soulful connection to all life.

Use the breath in every moment to pull you out of the limits of logic. The freer you become, the lighter you are, the more elevated your frequency, and your connection to those in spirit is clearer. Everything is energy. This entire human experience is a construct of a divine, intentional energy. You are a part of this universal field of consciousness. It is all available to you and beyond the limits of logic. The breath is beyond the confines of fear and beyond ego-mind identification.

## Conclusion

Now you know the real truth about the mystical and the scientific importance of Flattening your Abs with one breathing technique. Do Kapalabhati breathing every day.

## DR. KIM BYRD-RIDER, MPT, DPT, MPSYCH

### WHO IS DR. KIM?

Dr. Kim is a physical therapist and a psychologist. It was her privilege to have taught over 12,000 yoga classes before she acquired four science degrees in healthcare while working full-time in hospitals. View official resume/CV : https://www.byrdriderrehab.com/wp-content/uploads/2020/05/CV-Dr.-Kim-Byrd-Rider.pdf

- ♦ Master of Psychology – Harvard University, 2016-2020
- ♦ Doctor of Physical Therapy – Boston University, 2011-2014
- ♦ Master of Physical Therapy – University of Oklahoma, 2006-2009
- ♦ Bachelor of Health Science – University of Oklahoma, 2003-2006
- ♦ Non-Profit Business Management Cert.– Harvard University, 2018-2018

Building real-world applications out of theoretical ideas drives her. She spends many hours, and sheds blood, sweat, and tears into her books "The Therapy Bible on Yoga" https://thetherapybibleonyoga.com/, "Forward Head: the Evil Arch-Enemy: A therapeutic analysis at Forward Head Syndrome & how to correct it" on amazon, and in the making of the "Yoga Rx with Dr. Kim" video series for specific orthopedic, neurologic and psychological diagnoses. View those videos FREE on ROKU, Apple TV, and Well World Tv: https://www.byrdriderrehab.com/broadcasts/

### WHAT DOES DR. KIM DO?

By teaching holistic courses to healthcare workers and medical science courses to holistic healers, she fosters holistic and medical healthcare systems to cross-pollenate or blend together, forming a new, more-powerful comprehensive Utopian Healthcare system.

Find courses at https://www.byrdriderrehab.com/

The power of philanthropies and free education for all have moved her to found her own intergenerational healthcare nonprofit organization: http://byrd-riders-secret-garden.org/ and video/podcast series "Physics and the Jedi" available on ROKU, Apple TV, Well World Tv. Here the two worlds of science and old religions collide and merge: https://www.byrdriderrehab.com/broadcasts/

**DR. KIM'S GOALS & LEGACY**

Dr. Kim's goal is to bring lasting mental and physical health to the masses via the new Utopian Healthcare system. As the masses heal rapidly, they will begin creating World Health & World Peace, thus fulfilling the prophecy of the current Pope Francis, "This is not an Era of Change, this is the Change of an Era." If you need a safe physical therapy yoga class for a specific diagnoses, don't miss "Yoga Rx with Dr. Kim", also on the previous platforms.

# References

Deshmukh, S. V., & Bedekar, N. (2017). Effect of Kapalabhati pranayama on core strength in overweight individuals. *International Journal of Yoga*, 2(3), 50-51.

Ferla, L., Darski, C., Paiva, L. L., Sbruzzi, G., & Vieira, A. (2016). Synergism between abdominal and pelvic floor muscles in healthy women: a systematic review of observational studies. *Fisioterapia em Movimento*, 29(2), 399-410.

Jain, S. (2016). Effect of 6 weeks Kapalabhati pranayama training on pulmonary and cardiovascular parameters of young, prehypertensive obese medical students. *International Journal*, 5(4), 1471.

Qandeel, H., & O'Dwyer, P. J. (2016). Relationship between ventral hernia defect area and intra-abdominal pressure: dynamic in vivo measurement. *Surgical Endoscopy*, 30(4), 1480-1484.

# CHAPTER 10

# Qigong is the Way
## A Calming Practice for Health and Long Life

### BY RICHARD W. BREDESON

## My Story

### THE HEART OF A 20-YEAR OLD

It was August, 2017, about a week after my 72nd birthday. I was in the early stages of my Qigong strength training routine for cardio-fitness, doing my 100 pushups. And I felt a twinge I had not experienced before; in my chest. I continued on with my exercise, but I struggled a bit more than usual. And I was spent for the rest of the day.

My mother had had heart surgery in her mid-70s, so I was aware of my vulnerability. But this tightness, a bit of pain, a little shortness of breath, was surely not my heart. Besides, I had a Qigong class to teach the next day, my regular Friday class. I pressed on and taught my class, but this discomfort continued. And then it began to radiate, even spreading to my back, the area behind my heart. I took my wife's advice to get checked out!

Fast-forward: The urgent care EKG showed signs of a heart problem. The ER in Annapolis, Maryland measured a huge elevation in my troponin level, a clear marker for heart attack. No surgery in Annapolis on the weekend, so onward to an early Saturday morning ambulance ride to the Washington Medical Center (visibility too poor for a helicopter ride). Later Saturday morning, the emergency catheterization showed blockages in three arteries feeding my heart, requiring by-pass.

I was stable, comfortable, feeling okay after a rather undramatic heart attack, so they made me wait; there were other priorities for the six rooms dedicated to heart surgery operating at full capacity around the clock! They put me on the Tuesday schedule.

Meanwhile, waiting for my "team" to free up, I practiced Qigong. I found quiet, sunny spots and went through my favorite forms, getting my body ready for the invasive procedure. I wanted my mind as calm as possible as well. Nurses and staff were curious; they wanted to know more. "Do you teach?" they asked. "Maybe you could come back and teach here at the hospital."

Tuesday came, and I felt ready. I had my wife and some dear friends to hold the energy and space for my complete recovery. The worst part was waking up, still intubated; I fought the tube, part of me wanting to control my fear, vulnerability, and panic, part of me feeling weak that I could not, and then they put me out again. The best part was my recovery-room over-night nurse who cleaned me up and held me in such love; I will never forget that cared-for feeling of grace. I was alive.

I was home by Saturday afternoon, a fast recovery. As they were doing a final check on my readiness for release, the cardiologist who read my last echocardiogram pronounced, "You have the heart of a 20-year old. You just needed some plumbing work."

Within five months I went back to my Qigong strength training; I had to keep exercising that 20-year old heart! I still do this practice three times a week.

Everyone exclaimed over my recovery. A nurse friend visited with her stethoscope and blood pressure cuff. She examined my "zipper"—the scar left behind after they opened up my chest to perform the "triple CABG" procedure (Cardio Artery By-Pass Graft). She was stunned at the healing that had progressed so rapidly. She also happens to be one of my Qigong students and knew exactly how my body recovered so quickly and easily.

Qigong saved my life. Sure, I could have survived the heart attack without Qigong. Yes, I probably would have healed from surgery, eventually. But we don't know that for certain. What I do know is that I owe Qigong practice a forever debt of gratitude for my continued health, happiness, and expected long life. What I mean by this is I owe all the ancestors who carried their lineages forward across several thousand years. I owe all my teachers who continue those lineages and deep teachings. I owe my students for asking me to teach, the best way to learn anything. I owe my wife for her care, support, and encouragement. And I owe Laura Di Franco for inviting me to tell this story and teach this tool!

## The Tool

### EASY BONE MARROW WASHING

Qigong, Qi Gong, is a physical art form rooted in prehistory; it emerged as a practice out of the Shamanistic Path toward understanding the human condition. The term itself is relatively recent, used to convey a collection of practices documented as far back as 3000 years. The term is composed of two Chinese words: Qi meaning "energy," and "life force." This is the subtle energy of the body; most people feel it as goosebumps, shivers, hair standing on end. Qi can also mean "breath." Gong means "work" and "practice." It can also be translated as "cultivation." Putting these two words together, we get Qigong = Energy Practice, Breath Work, Life Force Cultivation.

The tool I offer you here is a Qigong Practice. We use the energy of the body, life force, Qi, to relax, inducing a feeling of calm, clearing not only the body but also the mind and spirit of any accumulated stress, worry, fear, anxiety, sadness, and anger. This is important because these stress factors harm our physical bodies; they are the major cause of disease. Now some stress is beneficial and necessary. When we are in danger and need to react quickly, our autonomic nervous system kicks in to save the day. Our adrenals pump out cortisol, a hormone that prepares the body to fight or flee or freeze, depending on the circumstances. In our modern relatively safe times, however, our sources of stress are not typically life-threatening. But the autonomic nervous system doesn't know this, so it often goes into hyperdrive overproducing cortisol, which builds up and overloads our systems. This build-up creates inflammation and is particularly harmful to our immune system. We want to reverse the effects of stress, moving into calm relaxation as regularly as we are able.

"Easy Bone Marrow Washing" is a tool you can learn and practice in five minutes. It can be done simply standing in one place or even sitting. I'll take you through the particulars in a simple step-by-step process. But first a word about breath. Now I realize if you have already read a couple of chapters in this volume, you will have noted the importance of breath. It is the basis for almost all healing techniques and practices that I'm aware of. Qigong practice is no exception.

To review briefly, Qigong breathing is belly breathing, abdominal breathing, inhaling deeply into the diaphragm. When we sit quietly and breathe into the lowest part of our body, expanding our belly out, like a "Buddha Belly," we begin to get the feel of it. Once our belly is extended, the breath continues to rise into the ribs and chest, the upper lung area. Our shoulders, ideally, do not rise; they may expand laterally a bit as the collarbone area relaxes. With practice, we can even bring the breath up into the throat, up the back of the neck, even as high as the top of the head. And our exhale reverses this as the air is relaxed out from the upper chest, down through the sternum area and back into the belly; we may even bring the abdomen back toward the spine, gently, to fully expel the breath to get ready for the next inhale.

This is typical Qigong breathing. It is always through the nose. It is quiet and gentle. The breath can be described as "long and slender." We use this breathing technique when practicing the tool. Let's go to the tool now:

1. We begin in a "rooted posture." This can be in either a standing or seated position. (When seated, choose a firm chair with no arms and a straight back; sit forward with feet firmly planted on the floor and plenty of space between your back and the chair.) Place your feet parallel, pointing straight ahead. Think about feeling rooted to the earth. Knees are relaxed, tailbone is pointed straight down, hips are open and broad, spine is straight, tucking the chin lifts the top of the head up toward the sky. Shoulders are broad, open, relaxed, soft. Hold the arms away from the body in a round shape. Fingers open and pointed down toward the "earth."

   Hold this posture throughout the practice, anchoring between the earth and sky. Move your attention inward; maybe even closing your eyes; feeling centered, grounded, present.

2. From this posture of open acceptance, we begin the practice and movement: your breath is coordinated with each movement. Inhale a long and slender breath, and bring your arms out, away from the sides of your body, palms facing up; it's like standing (or sitting) in a posture of receiving grace. Pause there, and exhale. You can hold this posture for several breaths, feeling the energy, accepting the energy of Heaven pouring down onto the palms of your hands, to the top of your head, into your whole body. This is the energy of the Sun, the Moon, the Planets and Stars, Celestial Energy, the gift of Heaven.

3. Take another breath in, and as you inhale, lift your hands up, still with the palms facing the sky, arching them up and then over your head where they hover above your brow-center. Fingertips are now aligned but not touching; palms are aimed at the forehead. Exhale here, sinking into the posture, pausing to feel and relax.

4. Next inhale again, filling with air and Qi and then slowly exhale while lowering the hands and arms, letting the palms sweep down along the front of the body, not touching, feeling the energy radiating out and downward from the palms along the entire front of the body. This is like scanning with "energy hands" from the top of your head to the tips of your toes. Your hands lower all the way down, past the waist, aiming down along the legs all the way to the feet. This is all in one long exhale. And then you return the hands to the sides where you began.

5. Breathe naturally, moving your attention inward as you sense how you feel. From here, you repeat this receiving, arching, scanning movement several times, at least three. After each repetition, pause and "check-in" with your mind, sensing how you're feeling at all levels: physically, emotionally, mentally, spiritually.

6. After several rounds of the practice and continuous mental, inward sensing of how you are doing, come to stillness and know you are complete. Close the practice in gratitude moving into a "prayer posture," hands and palms together, fingertips pointed upward, thumbs resting gently on the sternum, and hold this posture for at least three deep Qigong breaths.

It's that simple! With practice, we begin to feel lighter, connected, feet grounded to the earth with head in the clouds. I have called this "easy bone marrow washing" because it is a variation and a simplification of the classic form of Bone Marrow Washing. Yet while this practice is simple, easy enough for anyone to do, it is a deep practice. In Classic Chinese Medicine, the bones and the marrow are the deepest part of our energy anatomy. There are many layers to our energy bodies, and the more we practice with this tool, the deeper we can go in our clearing, relaxing, and healing work.

And for those who want to continue to go deeply with this practice here are just a few tips:

♦ When first beginning the practice, pausing in the "rooted posture," breathing rhythmically, intentionally, you can bring your attention inward and visualize an inner scan, almost like a mind's eye CT Scan, feeling your way along, from the toes upward along the entire body to the top of the head. And if there is something that catches your attention, maybe a tightness, a twitch, even a painful area, focus your attention there; it is a sign to work on that spot during your practice.

♦ At this beginning point, you also want to bring an intention to your practice. I've labeled this a "calming tool," and it is great for that. It can also be used for healing, for a standing, moving meditation, for praise and gratitude work, and grief work. Name the emotion, and this practice can transform it from its negative feeling to one of light and positivity.

♦ When standing in the receiving posture, arms out and palms up, you're accepting the Celestial Light and Energy of Heaven. Pause here in great gratitude.

♦ During the downward scan, hold your palms at a 45-degree angle to the body. Imagine rays of Qi-energy pouring out and down along the body as you lower your hands and arms during this long exhale. You're sending healing energy into the body and simultaneously purging any stress and negativity, you may be holding, sending it down into the earth to be composted.

♦ The closing in "prayer posture" is our time to give thanks. And following the quiet three breaths, we come back into our space, filled with energy, grounded in our bodies with a smile on our face!

May you use this simple tool with many blessings filled with love, light, and the healing grace of Heaven.

Richard W. Bredeson is both a technologist and a healer. He retired at the end of 2007, after nearly 40 years in the aerospace and communications industries applying software engineering, management, marketing, and sales skills. He went to "work" for his wife, Rosemary Robertson Bredeson, to bring her talents, skills, and healing power into the world. He maintains several websites for both their joint businesses, their church, and other non-profit organizations. Richard was ordained in 2000 as an Interfaith Minister by The Seminary of Pebble Hill Interfaith Community Church, Doylestown, PA. He and Rosemary provide "spiritual services" through their church, Church of A New Alliance, Inc., a 501(c)(3) non-profit organization: (http://ChurchofaNewAlliance. org) As a healer he studies, practices and teaches Qigong, an ancient Chinese approach to health, happiness, and longevity. Richard was certified to teach Qigong by Supreme Science Qigong Center in 2012. He has been researching, practicing, and teaching steadily since then. He teaches group classes every week; schedules are available on his Qigong website: https://QigongistheWay.com He is a member and webmaster of ACT (A Community of Transformation) a non-profit organization and a non-voting member of ACT's Co-Creation Council, the governing body of the organization. In 2019 he wrote a chapter in the best-selling collaborative book that describes the ACT governing approach: *Circular Leadership: Together We Rise*. Richard is also a poet working on several collections to be published soon; he sporadically publishes thoughts and poems on his blog: http://MenandtheGoddess.com.

If you want to receive a demonstration of Richard's "Easy Bone Marrow Washing Tool" described in this chapter, go to: https://QigongistheWay.com/Bone-Marrow-Washing.

# CHAPTER 11

# Finding Your Zen
## A Recipe for Natural Restoration No Matter Where You Live

### BY SUSAN AND JON CROSS

WARNING: Being part of nature creates a state of being and presence that improves your physical and mental health.

Nature has been called one of the world's best prescriptions for restoration by indigenous people, scholars, theologians, scientists, and artists since the beginning of time. What the typical nature Rx label doesn't tell you, however, is that this prescription isn't just a one-time experience. With regular use, it connects you with an unlimited energy source you can count on for personal restoration every time you let yourself become part of it.

There are literally thousands of white papers, blogs, videos, songs, great works of literature, and stories that document the benefits of time spent in nature. You can have

- ♦ A stronger body
- ♦ Improved memory
- ♦ Better problem-solving abilities
- ♦ Lower blood pressure
- ♦ Lower obesity rates
- ♦ More positive moods

♦ Less stress, anxiety, and depression
♦ Better focus

How does nature work its magic on us? It is the ultimate model for *being* and *presence*, two natural states that are essential for us to live purposeful, fulfilling lives, but sadly are often missing from the daily experiences of our all-too-busy world. Nature is always present as itself. It exists without pretense or apology in both the best and worst of times. It may be influenced by outside forces (like humans) trying to control it, but it still just "is."

When we connect with nature as a fundamental life force, we see ourselves as strong, capable, and resilient, just like it is. It's a connection that helps us see the world from a place of wonder and awe rather than fear and foreboding. We call this finding your Zen environment or *zenvironment* for short. A zenvironment is an intentional place of restoration, self-awareness, and calm attentiveness that allows us to find the peace we need to be better versions of ourselves. Best of all? Whether you live in the city, the suburbs, or the country, creating a personal zenvironment is easy when you follow the roadmap nature herself uses every day.

## Our Story

We've been married since 1985, and our lives have always been full of things we're "doing." We work, we've raised a family, we socialize, we travel, we meet deadlines, we agree, we disagree. The list goes on and on. We like to say that we've grown up together, especially since we had very different childhoods. Jon grew up in the country, Susan, in the suburbs. We've each always appreciated nature but experienced it differently. Jon was a dig-in-the-dirt kind of guy, making forts, hiking, collecting arrowheads, and exploring creeks. Susan mostly thought of nature as a place to go to for a specific reason like hiking, swimming, boating, and touring. Our different experiences complemented each other until the day we learned that our eight-acre woodlot was located in a rare natural habitat called The Oak Openings Region.

The Oak Openings Region is a tract of land a little larger than the state of Rhode Island between Toledo, Ohio, and Detroit, Michigan, that was formed by ancient glaciers. The Nature Conservancy has called the Oak Openings one of America's Last Great Places. It's as rare as the Everglades in Florida, the temperate rain forests of Washington state, and the Redwood Forests in California. About 99 percent is developed, and most people don't even realize they're in it. Some of the remaining one percent is owned by conservation parks, but the majority of what's left is hidden in the hands of private landowners, like us.

The story behind our property intrigued us on a personal level. Up until that point, it had always just been our homestead. It was an anchor for our family because we lived there, not because we felt any special natural connection to it. We pretty much let it grow wild except for the traditional grass lawn we'd carved out of the woods. Jon's casual attitude changed completely when we learned the history of where we lived. Actually, that's an understatement. He started to see our woods as a living breathing entity compelling him to bring it back to its native state. The man became obsessed.

The rest of our family thought he was just going all-in on another one of his projects, but we were wrong. He was on a mission. It made us wonder: Were we meant to be stewards of it and not just owners? Were the woods calling us to be part of something bigger than ourselves? For Susan and the kids, the initial answer was "No."

"I have to admit that when I first started the restoration journey, I took it on as a project," said Jon. "The more I worked on it, though, the more I became convinced that it was actually part of my life's purpose. I wasn't sure why, but I just knew. And, I felt better about myself just thinking about what might be possible."

To the average eye, our property just looked like thick woods. From a native state perspective, it was an overgrown mess. Large, non-native trees had created a canopy that choked out the sun and sucked up the natural resources in the soil so that the native plants couldn't grow. What we later learned was a rare buttonbush swamp looked more like a big mud hole filled with decaying leaves and smelly muck rather than water and life. Restoring the woods to its native state would take years and repeated disruption that cleared away anything that wasn't supposed to be there so that the property's natural state of being could return and thrive.

Natural restoration is not for the faint of heart, and it's not pretty. For 12 years, we watched Jon cut down large healthy trees that weren't native to our area to open the woods to the sun. We fought off fear when he set the woods on fire in an annual series of controlled burns that literally charred all of the undergrowth on the property down to ugly, smelly ashes (the native trees were unharmed). We laughed as he waded into the swamp in hip boots to clear out debris clogging the natural flow of the water.

Jon, actually, has had the last laugh. The results of his conservation and restoration efforts have been spectacular! Our 12-year journey has not been a straight line, but we've successfully brought back many rare plants and species—some that had been considered near extinction in our area. What surprised us the most is that we didn't have to plant many seeds. We just had to eliminate invasive species and disrupt the wrong environment to give what's supposed to be there a chance to thrive—a shot at being and presence.

Our nature "show" now includes a fully restored native habitat that supports wildflowers and rare orchids, plants and sedge grasses, songbirds of all sizes and colors, owls, hawks, choruses of frogs, fox, deer, wild turkeys, wood ducks and mallards, dragonflies, butterflies, salamanders, turtles, and a full spectrum of seasonal colors. On any given day, we can immerse ourselves in a full-on sensory experience of natural sights, sounds, smells, touch, and taste that make us feel calmer and steadier simply because they exist.

Susan experienced the benefits of our zenvironment when she faced a lengthy and challenging recovery from a medical emergency.

"I nearly died when my appendix ruptured while on vacation on a remote Caribbean island," she said. "It was the biggest disruption of my life and forced me into a different state of normal. I startled easily. I experienced PTSD. I had trouble saying complete sentences. What helped my recovery was retreating into our woods and letting the energy powering its native state of being surround me and help me heal. It was the beginning of my rediscovery of me. I slowed down. My breathing became more regular. My brain fog cleared. I was able to increase my stamina. It was as if nature took hold of me and pushed me forward a little at a time. Nature helped me create my own zenvironment and a renewed sense of purpose."

You might say that we've become hooked on nature. The successful restoration of our initial eight-acre woodlot has led to the restoration of a 12-acre wet prairie. In fact, when we first walked the prairie before we purchased it, we looked at each other with wide eyes and acknowledged that we felt its lifeforce under our feet. It was as if the property was calling out to us for help so that it could be its best self.

The process for restoring our property has become a metaphor for the intentionality by which we now live our lives. We've witnessed firsthand that nature doesn't stop because invasives have taken hold. It waits, patiently, until someone or something disrupts what's not supposed to be there and makes way for its true self to grow with presence and being. Nature's state of being and presence has become us.

## The Tools

### PART 1: FOLLOW NATURE'S RECIPE FOR RESTORATION

To rediscover yourself and take advantage of all that nature has to teach us, follow what we call "nature's recipe for restoration." These are the basic steps we took when we restored our property.

1.  Identify the invasives in your life. What's getting in the way of you being your best self? Is it a job situation that isn't working? Are you in a bad relationship? Write these down. Choose one or two to remove at a time—you don't have to

do it all. We would have been overwhelmed if we'd tried to tackle everything at once. To this day, we work on small sections over time.

2.  Be brave enough to own what you love about yourself. This is not an act of arrogance. It's self-indulgence and grace of the best kind. Nature showcases its glory every chance it gets. Think about birds flying south in a perfect V-formation, a flower growing in the crack of a sidewalk, or the quiet sound of snow falling in the early morning before the noises of the day get going. Are you taking time to notice the beautiful natural images and sounds that are uniquely you? What makes your heart sing? What is it that makes you uniquely you that maybe you are afraid to move forward with? Challenge yourself to list at least five things you love about yourself. We think you'll learn to list even more!

3.  Welcome a little prescribed disruption in your environment, even if it's painful or scary. What are you willing to change? This is the hard part. Remember the story of the controlled fires? Write down one change you can make to your current situation to help you get rid of the invasives in your life. Then, do it! Take the first step to fix or get out of a bad relationship or job situation. Embrace the disruption that may happen. Consider it an opportunity to be a better you. Seek help from friends and professionals. You don't have to do this alone!

4.  Show up for yourself every day. You don't have to be perfect. Life is in a constant state of change, and everything is imperfect, impermanent, and incomplete. Nature is in a constant of transition and it's beautiful, just like you. Start small with a simple daily mantra or prayer that acknowledges your presence and state of being. Sit comfortably with both feet flat on the floor or ground. Open a window or listen to a recording of birds, water flowing, wind, rain, or something similar and let the natural sounds surround you. Close your eyes. Quiet your mind focusing on your

breathing. Count to four as you breathe in. Count to four as you exhale. Keep this up for two minutes. (Set a timer if you need to.)

5. Step back when all the hard work is done, smile, and celebrate. We know that amazing things will unfold all around you.

## PART 2: SPEND TIME WITH NATURE

Need to start a little smaller? It doesn't take restoring a natural habitat to become part of the presence and being of nature. The first step to becoming part of nature is to step into it. Here are 20 simple ways you can spend time with nature and improve your mood through presence and being.

1. Use your legs to hike or bike for 30 minutes.
2. Train to become a trail guide with your local park system.
3. Visit public wilderness spaces.
4. Follow animal tracks.
5. Volunteer to tend an urban garden.
6. Plant herbs.
7. Grow a garden.
8. Bring flowers indoors.
9. Play in the dirt.
10. Go barefoot.
11. Eat seasonal foods grown locally. Pick them yourself when possible.
12. Spend time near water.
13. Sit by an open window or outside, close your eyes and listen to birds.
14. Take a deep breath every time you walk outside. Hold for 4 seconds and release. Repeat twice.
15. Use your tech to store birds singing or water flowing. Make nature photos your screen savers and home or lock screens.
16. Take one nature photo a day and share it with someone else.

17. Watch a sunrise or sunset.
18. Join a local walking or hiking club.
19. Volunteer to collect native seeds with your local parks or nature associations.
20. Stop talking and listen to the natural sounds around you for 1 minute every day. Set a timer if needed.

**ABOUT US**

Susan and Jon Cross are passionate advocates of connecting with nature to reduce stress and anxiety and improve mood. They call this experience creating a Zen environment or zenvironment for short. They're on a mission to help others create their own zenvironments and experience firsthand the healing power and grounding of nature. Susan and Jon help people and nature through writing and speaking and through their front-line preservation activities in the rare habitat where they live, The Oak Openings Region in Ohio.

Their family includes four amazing children/children-in-law, one grand-cat, and two grand-pups. When not tending to their own zenvironment, they can be found hiking, traveling, cooking (and eating), researching family history, and inspiring people to see the world in powerful new ways via their alter egos. Susan is a published author and public relations expert. Jon is a highly regarded Oak Openings Region nature conservationist and information technology leader.

www.zenvironment.life; www.susan-cross.com

# CHAPTER 12

# Imagination
## The First Steps to Your Best Self

### BY DOUGLAS RUARK

## My Story

Back in 2014, I had a wonderful job in communications in San Francisco. During the summer of that year, I was asked by friends to go with them in the early fall to do some outreach work at an elementary school in Nepal and then to climb Mt. Everest. "No way," I said immediately. I couldn't imagine myself climbing up a mountain, living in a tent, and not being able to shower for 11 days. As time passed, the thought of this adventure wouldn't leave my mind, and I kept hearing a small voice inside me saying, *this is something you have to do. It's going to change your life, it's going to be amazing, and it's an opportunity of a lifetime.* After fighting it for several weeks, I decided to go. I quit my job, and with a lot of nerves and excitement, headed off to Katmandu, Nepal.

The outreach work at the elementary school was an amazing and fulfilling experience. Before leaving for Nepal, we had received many generous donations, which allowed us to purchase new school supplies for every child in the school. We were also able to put in new floors, a new irrigation system, and some fun play equipment for the schoolyard. Every time we helped in any way, we were always thanked by the children putting their hands together and bowing. I felt like I was being blessed all the time. Once we completed our outreach work, it was tough to say goodbye.

A few days after the outreach work was completed, my friends and I began our 11-day trek up Everest to Basecamp. I was filled with awe, beginning with my very first step up the mountain. I was the oldest in the group by about 20 years. My friends were amazed that I never used my walking sticks all the way up. They asked me, "What keeps you motivated, Douglas?" For some of them, it was challenging. "I'm not thinking so much about the climb," I replied, "I imagine the mountain as a metaphor for my life." I could envision my life changing with every summit I reached, and I knew without a doubt that the views would be spectacular and something I never would have imagined. I walked up Everest in awe and amazement. I made it all the way up, whereas one of my friends had to be taken down by helicopter because for him it was a difficult journey in his head. I chose to take the trip up the mountain in my imagination.

Before arriving back home in San Francisco, I knew I had to do something different with my life. I had looked at life coaching and found out a certification was being held in San Diego the following week. I registered immediately, booked my flight and hotel, and a few days later, I was in San Diego for a week of workshops and classes. I received my certification, and my first two clients were students in the class with me. They are still my clients, and they view me as part of their success team.

I hope my story will inspire you to use the natural-born gift of your imagination to take steps to your best self.

## The Tool: Imagination

What do you want your life to be like? Are you spending your time thinking about what is right, or what could go wrong? Are you spending time each day imagining a life that has you excited to wake up each morning? Imagine what might happen if you dedicate some time seeing yourself taking steps to your best self.

Albert Einstein said: "Imagination is more important than knowledge. For while knowledge defines all we currently know and understand, imagination points to all we might yet discover and create." You use your imagination all the time, whether you are conscious of it or not. For example, there is a great job opening in your field. What is your first thought? Is it, *I would be perfect for that job*? Can you imagine yourself getting the job, showing up for work, and loving what you do? Or, do you tell yourself all the reasons why you won't get the job? Are you using your imagination, which you're born and wired with, to shape your best self?

Children use their imagination naturally, for fun. They seem to know intuitively that their imagination is a special gift. Within a few minutes, they pretend to be superheroes, doctors and nurses, and even a princess or a policeman. Unfortunately, as we grow up, well-meaning adults teach us to stop imagining and to stop playing. It's time to get more serious and to grow up. We now know that imagination is crucial to our creative process and to actively seeking our highest expression. Imagination is your gateway to reality.

The first step to your best self is a writing assignment, and it requires that you tell the truth to yourself about yourself. Healing and moving forward can't happen in a fantasy. This first step can sometimes be a little challenging, but it's well worth your effort. How do you view your life at this moment? Does a new day have you looking at your life through a new lens of opportunity and possibilities, or do you see the new day as not much different than yesterday? This first step requires your time, your honesty, and please try not to judge yourself. It's important to remember you've done your best up to this point with what you know.

Schedule some time away from all the noise and settle down in your favorite spot. Light a candle, make yourself a wonderful cup of tea, grab your paper and some colored pencils (I suggest colored pencils to have the play begin), and allow yourself to get ready to spend some quality time with yourself. You may even choose to say a prayer, meditate, play, or simply sit in silence for a few minutes before you start writing. Has it been a while since you spent some quality time with yourself? Enjoy this time!

As you begin to reflect, here are a few questions to help you get started: Do I always put others first and myself last? How do I see my health? How do I see my income? How do I see my vocation? What gives my life meaning, and am I bringing that forth now? What brings me joy, and am I allowing it now? What was my favorite thing to do as a child? What do I wish I had more time to do? When is the last time I felt lit-up? What desires do I have that keep tugging at my heart that I'm not fulfilling? What would I do if I didn't care what others thought? Do I feel like I deserve the best?

You may even be saying that your life is wonderful and fulfilling, but that you still may feel like a little something is missing. You may want to ask yourself some of the following questions: Why am I here in this moment? Why am I here in this lifetime? What are my gifts and talents? What do I want more of in my life? Is there anything that I'm not doing because of fear? What would give me peace of mind?

Spend as much time as you need with this first step. It's a powerful step and a wonderful beginning. Dive as deeply as you are comfortable doing in this moment. You can always go back to this process any time you choose. What you have decided to do here is a precious gift to yourself. It's intended for your eyes only, and you never need to share it with another person. If you choose to share it with someone else, please make sure you trust them completely, and they have your best interest at heart.

Now would be the perfect time to breathe, relax, and let go of any need to do this right or try to control it. The next steps you are about to take are the beginning of where you can imagine your life and the world around you a little differently. Imagine yourself living on the bottom level of an apartment building, and you're getting ready to move up to the second floor. On the first floor, all you can see is the street in front of you and possibly the building next door. On the second floor, you can see you are part of a neighborhood, and there is a park nearby. As you begin to take steps forward, your view of yourself and your possibilities will expand.

Here is where you begin to reveal what's on your list and what's important to you. You're not starting to make changes yet. You'll begin to make changes a little later. Let's examine a few scenarios I see in my coaching practice:

Scenario #1—You're extremely concerned about your health, and your doctor has told you that your weight is a concern. He's prescribed high blood pressure medication, and you're afraid of the long-term side effects. You're always tired and have no energy. It's hard for you to find clothes that you like or fit you right. You feel embarrassed to be around your friends, family, and co-workers. When you're out in public, you catch people pointing and laughing at you. You keep to yourself and have no social life. You've been diagnosed with depression, and you're taking medication for that as well.

Scenario #2—You're unhappy with your life, and it feels empty. The dream you've always had is to write and publish a children's book, and the story has been in your head for at least ten years. It feels like the dream is slipping away. You've never shared your dream with anyone. You're the breadwinner in your family, and you always make them the priority. They think you're doing just fine because you have a hard time sharing your feelings. Writing a book and having it published is always on your mind and what it could mean for your family.

Scenario #3—You've always dreamed of opening your own healing business, but you don't know where to start. People will think you're crazy because you have a great job. The customers won't come. Your family won't support you, so you've never mentioned it to them. Security is important to you and your family. You're afraid of failure, and not sure you have the stamina or skills required to run your own business.

This next step is where I would ask you to allow in some play and creativity. You may say that play is for children, but as you're taking steps forward to your best self, being childlike allows you to possess the purity of the heart and mind, and the consciousness of the truth that anything is possible. It fosters your imagination and creativity. Imagination was given to us in our fairy tales: *The Little Engine That Could*, "I think I can, I think I can." *Cinderella*, "It's possible for a plain yellow pumpkin to become a golden carriage. It's possible." Don't you still believe in fairy tales? The more you can relax and enjoy the process that's beginning to unfold before you, the more you will be willing to keep taking steps to your best self.

Simply play along with me and imagine your life without the concerns you've mentioned. This can be a challenge because sometimes it's hard to see past the current self and to see what's possible. But with some gentle nudging and questions pertaining to what's been written down, eventually, everyone begins to open up and relax. When a client begins to imagine a life that's different, what I witness happening very quickly in front of me is a change in their body posture, lightness and playfulness beginning to emerge, and a change in their energy. It's amazing, yet nothing has changed other than allowing their imagination to run wild and free and to play.

Scenario #1—Next Step. You're at your ideal weight and feeling great. You've joined a gym, and you love exercising, and you're not taking any medications. Shopping is enjoyable, and you always find clothes that fit and are beautiful. You have a partner now, and love spending time with your family and friends socializing and having fun. At work, you've received a promotion, and you love your new job and the people you work with. You're very happy and satisfied with your life.

Scenario #2—Next Step. Your children's book has been published, and you're thrilled. There is a great sense of accomplishment and pride in writing a children's book in Spanish that is being well received and filling a need in the market. You speak and do readings all over the world and have won several literary awards for your writing. You're working on your second book. Recently, you were approached to perhaps have your book become a children's TV show. You feel like anything is possible, and you're doing exactly what you're meant to do in life.

Scenario #3—Next Step. Your healing business is open, and it's very successful. You love owning your own business, and your family supports you 100%. Lots of people have stepped forward to help you because they believe in you. Getting the funding was easy. You are thinking about expansion plans. You've put a down payment on a beach house that you've always dreamed about.

The steps going forward are about taking action and starting to make some small changes and building from there. It's about taking baby steps and cheering yourself along the way. Making small changes will boost your confidence and encourage you to take steps to your best self.

Scenario #1—Possible Next Steps. Reach out and seek professional guidance on beginning a walking program. Make an appointment with a nutritionist to get assistance with a healthy eating program. Join a meditation class to enhance your mindset and belief in yourself. Ask for support from your family and friends.

Scenario #2—Possible Next Steps. Sit down with your family and let them in on your dream for writing a book and ask for their support. Go to the store and buy a beautiful diary and pen and begin writing. Schedule writing time in your schedule every day.

Scenario #3—Possible Next Steps. Again, always be honest with your family and ask for their support. Get a mentor. Attend workshops on opening a business. Start researching funding options.

I'm grateful you took the time to read about how the power of your imagination can assist you in taking steps forward to your best self. Keep going, and remember, you will always tend to act like the person you conceive yourself to be. What you're holding in your mind and heart creates your world. So, what kind of world do you want to create? You can start harnessing the amazing power of your imagination not by trying to make things right but by seeing and feeling them rightly. When you see and feel things differently and behave differently, you change everything. Imagination is more important now than ever.

Douglas Ruark lives in San Francisco and loves his life coaching work with his clients. He feels like his calling in life is to help others. Douglas believes in having a morning routine, which for him includes getting up at 5:00 a.m. every day to meditate, write, have a great cup of coffee, feel the cool breeze coming in the open windows, watch the sunrise, and doing his 300 pushups. He shares his morning writings on his Facebook page, *My Wish for You Today*. Also, Douglas is the host of a weekly Zoom show called #CoffeeTalkWithDouglas. The guests on the show provide the audience with sound bowl meditations, cooking classes, a rose garden tour, angel card readings, poetry readings, concerts, creative writing, and discussions on prayer and many other topics.

Douglas has written several articles for *The Wellbeing World Journal* on love, courage, and his life-changing experience of climbing Mt. Everest. He is currently working on a children's book series and several other projects. He can be seen walking the hills of San Francisco daily and taking photographs of beautiful flowers. You can reach Douglas at douglasruark@gmail.com.

# CHAPTER 13

# Foam Rolling
## The Power to Move with Strength, Courage, and Confidence

### BY STACEY SIEKMAN, CLC

## My Story

The tragic and life-changing moment came for me when I was four months pregnant with my second child. The phone rang. "Your mom collapsed. She's had a massive stroke. You need to come." I felt like an enormous wave of darkness had suddenly and completely washed over me, making it difficult to breathe. As I stood with the phone in my hand, I thought, *I just talked to her two hours ago. This can't be real. She is healthy and strong. We just finished a half-marathon last month. Will she be able to talk or walk? Will she make it?* Thoughts, fears, and questions whipped around, leaving me in a mental state of utter chaos, not sure what to do, where to go, or who to call.

The long drive to the hospital was in slow motion, the questions, the anticipation, uncertainty, anxiety, all the intense emotions, stress, and fear rushed through my mind. *What will she look like? Will she need a wheelchair? Will she be able to feed herself? How will we care for her? Is she in pain? Will she recognize me? The baby?* A sense of panic seized my body when I walked into the

ER, slowing my steps as I approached the right side of the bed. My mom was lying on her back with her head turned away from me. "Mom, I'm here. It's okay, I am here." "She can't hear you from that side," the nurse said. As I walked around to the other side of the bed, I saw her troubled face dazed and confused, with a glazed look in her eyes.

Hearing my voice, she reached out to touch my pregnant stomach, unable to speak, but her words were spoken through her touch. She started to pull herself out of bed, and I could tell she was uncomfortable and scared. It was like her words were screaming from the inside with no sound on the outside. I kept saying, "Mom, you can't get out of bed." She kept trying. She wanted to get up, but her legs wouldn't move. I could sense her frustration and fear of not understanding why she couldn't get up, why her lower body wasn't responding to what she was trying to do. She was trapped inside a body that wouldn't move. I was desperately trying to calm her down, finally asking, "Do you need to go to the bathroom?" She nodded her head yes, her unspoken words and her internal discomfort and struggle finally being heard and seen. I called the nurses, and she was finally able to get relief. She settled down in the bed and closed her eyes.

Three days after the stroke, the neurosurgeon told my brother and me, "Your mom has lost her life skills and her ability to function as a human being. At best, she would be on a feeding tube for the rest of her life." We knew this is not what she would have wanted; it was time to move her to hospice.

Time ceased to exist; the seconds, minutes, hours, and days pooled together like a body of dark, still water. My mom's precious time on earth was coming to an end; her body was beginning to shut down. My family stood around her bedside to let her know, "It's okay, Mom; everyone is okay." We wanted her to let go and rest in peace.

The next morning, I witnessed my mom taking her last breath, her final "piece" of eternal peace. It was such an amazing gift to see, but a difficult gift to receive. Time stopped; my body felt numb, my life motionless. Death had taken over outside. I found myself drowning in a sea of darkness, staring at an image, a reflection, unrecognizable, uncertain, without definition, purpose, or movement. But at the same time, life was still moving inside. I had a new life inside of me; a baby, developing, growing; clearly defined with purpose and intentional movement. An intense emotional struggle took place on the outside, yet there was a strong connection of image, truth, and life on the inside. As life ended for my mom, life was developing for my daughter, and *beginning* for me.

So many thoughts and questions rushed through my mind; death on the outside, life on the inside. *What is happening? Where do I go? What do I do? Will I be defined and destroyed by death on the outside, or will I stay connected and committed to life on the inside? How do I nourish and protect the life growing inside of me when the external world around me is beating me up?* I had to maintain balance in my body in order to nourish, cherish, and protect the life inside me. I moved from an external search to an internal journey. The only way out of the darkness was to seek the truth behind my reflection. This was a truth that could only be found deep inside the life I carried; a life that had a significant purpose, a life that needed proper rest, a life that needed to be nourished, and a life with movement; the life of my baby. My unborn baby forced me to look at my own "life" inside; the "life" I carry around every day, the "life" that needs nourishment and rest, the place where my truth resides. This "life" is my **heart.** We always have a life dependent on us, the one within us, our **heart,** the *only* movement that matters, always until the day it stops! (This section was taken from my book *Coming Out of the Water: One HEART.*)

## MY POWER-FULL TURNING POINT

In a single moment, I stood face-to-face with death on the outside while carrying and experiencing life on the inside. I was caught at the precise point where the external and internal worlds collide. I knew I had a decision to make. I could keep my attention on the darkness and stillness of death on the outside, or I could turn my attention to the brightness and movement of life on the inside. This was not a life-defining moment, but a life-creating moment. My mom's death breathed life into the development of the Intentional Movement Coaching Series, H.I.T. Excellence and the Functional Core Training Programs, Core-Sage™, "t" Training®, and Tiny "t" Training®. I invite you to learn more about my programs by visiting www.balancedbodyreflections.com/.

This collision of life and death revealed this profound truth; that life doesn't happen to us; it happens for us. It is all about intention; what we see and how we move will directly impact the way we live.

Intentional Movement is not just about the physical work; it is about the internal deep core work, the HEART work. HEART work is the HARD work. Our heart, like my unborn child, is the "life" we carry inside of us. It needs more than just our attention; it needs our intention; our love, nurture, and support to not just survive, but to live. This work is not for those who merely exist; it's for those who want to truly live life with joy, intentionality, and purpose.

One of the tools of my program that I am extremely passionate about is Foam Rolling. This is used for connecting, balancing, and experiencing the Power in YOU! It is a profound way for you to learn how to move with strength, courage, and confidence.

## The Tool

*What you will need*: a PB Elite Molded Foam Roller (3' Long, 6" Round)

The foam roll is not just a tool; it is a tangible instrument that can be used to experience a deeper connection to the Power in You. It is a personal investment with a Power-FULL return!

(Invest in a Foam Roller here: www.balancedbodyreflections. com/resources)

**If you do not have a Foam Roll—you will still be able to participate in the movements**

## "LET'S ROLL!"

I invite you to find a comfortable, quiet, and open space on the floor.

Place the foam roll on the floor (carpet, wood, cement, tile—or any firm surface).

If you do not have a foam roll, you will be lying down on the floor.

### *Positioning*

First, you are going to sit at the very end of the foam roll. As you lay your back down on the foam roll, you will need to scoot your tail bone down to the very end of it. As one of my clients said while laughing, "It is like when you are at the gynecologist's office, and you have to keep scooting down farther and farther until you are at the very end of the table."

Your tailbone, back, and your head will be on the foam roll. Your knees will be slightly bent, with your feet firmly planted on the ground and your arms at your side with your hands resting on the ground, palms facing up.

If you are lying on the floor, I want you to visualize your spine as the foam roll. Picture yourself balancing on your spine. (The foam roll will give you a better experience with the concept of connecting and balancing.)

Second, allow yourself to BE STILL, sinking into your spine and all the way down into your heels as you experience being connected and grounded. Become aware of your breathing, your chest opening, stretching, and expanding with every breath.

Lastly, give your spine an energetic "hug," moving the energy from the top of your head all the way through your tail bone and down into your heels. I want you to think about wrapping the energy all the way around your spine, giving it a great big squeeze. Notice how this feels as you experience the deep connection to the core of being you. As you release the energetic "hug," let go of anything that is being carried, held, or stored inside. How is your body feeling now? (You may feel open, light, heavy, relaxed, tight, sore, or like your "floating")

This energetic "hug" of the spine is powerful and can be practiced anywhere at any time. It is a quick and easy way to disengage from the world and intentionally connect to your own energy, power, and strength. It will bring you into a powerful state of being---connected, balanced, controlled, and prepared to move!

## Connecting

Let's start by taking your left hand and placing it under your lower back. There is a space or an arch between the lower back and the foam roll (or ground). This is a critical area (or space) that will need to be intentionally connected. Many of us move through our lives disconnected from our own power. This is just one example of this.

I will be teaching you two intentional movements that are essential to connecting to the Power in You: The Pelvic Tilt and the Shoulder Blades into Hip Pockets.

1. **Pelvic Tilt:** The pelvic tilt closes the space between the lower back and the foam roll or the surface you are laying on. You are going to do a pelvic tilt by rolling the pelvis (hip bones) up towards your belly button (without lifting the hips off the foam roll) and HOLD this position for 5-10 seconds. This will flatten out your back while engaging the abs (be sure you are breathing, chest open, arms, legs, and neck, and head are relaxed.)

   While holding the pelvic tilt, take your left hand and try to put it under your back. There should not be any space. If there is, retry the pelvic tilt again until there is no space.

   Release the pelvic tilt. Notice how the space opens in the lower back area, disconnecting from the foam roll.
   Repeat the pelvic tilt and HOLD for 5-10 seconds. Your abs

are fully engaged. Experience the feeling of being connected to your own core strength, just by doing this small intentional movement. Without releasing the pelvic tilt, try to relax the rest of your body. Now, release the pelvic tilt again. (Describe your experience---ex. "I felt lighter in my legs and experienced an energy surge that ran up through my neck and out the top of my head.")

2. **Shoulder Blades into Hip Pockets:** The movement of pulling your shoulder blades straight down into your hip pockets helps to fully engage your core and will also help with your balance. Try pulling your shoulder blades straight down into your hip pockets, as far and as deep as you can, and HOLD for 5-10 seconds. While holding your shoulder blades down inside your hip pockets, gently squeeze the foam roll between your shoulder blades. You will feel a gentle stretch and opening across the chest and shoulder area. The combination of these two movements will open space between your ears and shoulders. *It is like you are coming out of your shell!*

   Release the shoulder blades. How did that feel? You may feel like you have a little less control when your shoulder blades are released. You may even notice that your shoulders are creeping their way back up towards your ears.

   Repeat pulling your shoulder blades down into your hip pockets as you gently squeeze the foam roll between your shoulder blades and HOLD for 5-10 seconds. Experience the feeling of being connected, balanced, and controlled by doing these two small intentional movements. While holding, try releasing and relaxing everywhere else, except this deep connection to the inside of you. Now, release the shoulder blades. (Describe your experience---ex. "I feel open, calm, and a little bit taller.")

3. **Connecting 1 & 2:** Now, let's put these movements together! Do the pelvic tilt AND pull the shoulder blades down into your hip pockets with a gentle squeeze of the foam roll between your shoulder blades and HOLD for 5-10 seconds. This is the core area that holds the POWER in YOU! This internal power is what we are going to connect to, balance with, and learn to use to move in a Power-FULL new way!

Release both and describe how you feel.

Repeat the two intentional movements and allow yourself to experience your power within. Describe your experience. I had a group of women on their foam rolls, and one of the women connected and experienced her internal power, which sent a powerful surge of energy through the room, causing me to have goosebumps and chills as she connected, and gasped. "I feel it, this is it!" I said, "YES, that is the POWER in YOU!" It brings tears to my eyes and goosebumps to my legs as I write these words because I can still feel the positively charged energy that was released when she connected to her power. It was an exhilarating experience for me, my client, and the other women in the room.

I invite you to connect to the POWER in YOU! It does not demand your attention; it requires your INTENTION to move and live with strength, courage, and confidence.

If you would like to watch a complete instructional video on foam rolling, please go to my resources page: www.balancedbodyreflections.com/resources.

Stacey Siekman is a Certified Life and Intentional Movement Coach, the Owner of Balanced Body Reflections, and Author of *Coming Out of the Water: One HEART*.

Stacey is the Founder of the Intentional Movement and Coaching Series: H.I.T. Excellence and the Functional Core Training Programs: Core-Sage™, "t" Training®, and Tiny "t" Training®. These combined with her competitive athletic background, along with 30+ years of coaching/teaching experience, working as a licensed massage therapist for 14 years, and her extensive fitness and nutritional knowledge provides her an incredible abundance of wisdom, knowledge, and experience in teaching and training women to move with strength, courage, and confidence through their middle-aged years.

If you are ready to move in a Power-FULL new way, Stacey would love to hear from you!

You are invited to connect with Stacey at:
https://www.balancedbodyreflections.com/
stacey@balancedbodyreflections.com
602-332-1908

You are welcome to join her FREE FB Group:
https://www.facebook.com/groups/
BalancedbodyreflectionsIntentionalHearts/

# CHAPTER 14

# Stress Relief
## Using Energy Healing for Optimal Health

### BY PAM BOHLKEN, REIKI MASTER, VSTP, RTTP

The best and most efficient pharmacy
is within your own system.
—Robert C. Peale

## My Story

Do you believe in Divine timing, that things happen for a reason? I do. In 2012 my niece had made appointments for herself, two of my sisters, and me to have readings done by an Intuitive Medium. I've always been interested in that type of thing, so I jumped on board. My sisters and my niece had what I would call normal readings. You know the type you hear about your kids, husbands, and grandkids? When I had my reading, I walked out of there in a daze. She told me, "You're a strong healer, and you'll be trained at Level 3 in Reiki within 18 months." I wasn't expecting that. I didn't even know what Reiki was. I went home and started to search for a book on Reiki. After reading the book, the only thing I could say was, *why isn't everyone doing this?* The biggest thing I learned was that by going into this deep relaxed state, it reduces stress in our bodies, while helping our body to heal itself.

I started the search for a Reiki instructor. From what I hear, I was doing this all backward. Normally people experience Reiki and then want to learn how to do it. I went into my first class without ever experiencing a session. I heard the instructor say, "You're a natural!" At that point, I was armed with these newly heated up hands that wanted to heal everyone and everything. You have to learn to control yourself because ethically you have to wait to be asked to do a healing. People give you a funny look if you just start placing your hands on them. I didn't quite get to Level 3 in 18 months, but that was because I put it off intentionally. I'm a little stubborn that way.

I continued to learn other forms of energy healing through very reputable healers like Echo Bodine, Annette Bruchu, and Donna Eden. I learned a few new techniques, but ultimately it comes down to me being a channel for the healing energy to come through me from the Universe to the client or myself.

In the fall of 2014, I found out one of the reasons I was brought into the Reiki world. I was experiencing pain in my right hip, and then it started in my left arm. I had gone to the doctor, but other than an abnormal blood test, she didn't really find anything and said, "Come back next month for more blood work, and we'll see if there's something else going on." When I got up one morning, a couple of weeks later, I couldn't get dressed. My arm wasn't working. I called into work requesting a sick day. Little did I know that one sick day would turn into nine months. I called the clinic to talk to my doctor, but I was told, "She's not in the office today."

I decided to soak in a hot tub and let my body relax. That felt really good, but when I stood up to take a shower to wash my hair, I ended up passing out. Once I came to, I heard my husband come into the house. I called out, "Dave, I need help." With my arm not working, I wasn't able to help myself out of the tub. My husband struggled unsuccessfully to get me out. I told him, "Call 911." Soon we had three first responders at the door. I'm not a big gal, but the position was awkward, and they had trouble too. My husband had gotten me a blanket, so I was covered up, but one of the guys finally had to step into the tub to get me out. As I was experiencing my first ride in an ambulance, I remember saying, "The hardest part is over," but I know the first responder knew better. In the emergency room, they said, "Your arm is broken." I was very surprised. I was 57 years old and had never broken a bone before. Then I had another surprise. The doctor said, "There is definitely something else going on. We need to have more tests done before we can know for sure. But first, we need to get that arm taken care of." I was sent to a different hospital where they could do more tests, and I could have surgery on my arm. During this hospital stay, I was introduced to an Oncologist. Yes, I had cancer. I was told I had Multiple Myeloma, and this lovely doctor told me, "You could live a good five to ten years with this."

At that point, I wasn't even sure what Multiple Myeloma was. I remember looking at my husband and asking him, "What did he just say? Am I going to die?" I had my surgery; I then had radiation to make sure the cancer was gone in my arm. From my understanding, Multiple Myeloma is a cancer of the blood, but then it starts eating away at your bones as it advances. My arm had been deteriorating, and that's where my pain was coming from. Then it was time for chemo. At this point, I'm on my third doctor. I started chemo; it went pretty well. I didn't lose my hair or get sick, so I count that as pretty good. At one of my chemo sessions, I was listening to my music and imagining that I was dancing with my spirit guides, angels, and Jesus. I remember thinking *Jesus is a pretty good dancer*. I was dancing along with them in my chair, and the nurse came over to check on me. Apparently, I was moving around in my chair so much she thought I might be having a seizure. I wasn't. It was just my way of getting through the chemo session. Chemo was going so well that my oncologist said he didn't see any reason to continue. My next step was a stem cell transplant.

Having a stem cell transplant was a whole different ballgame. I went to the U of M in Minnesota for the procedure. I then had to stay on campus at the Hope Lodge for the next month so that

I could be close by for my daily appointments and in case of an emergency. I had to have a caregiver with me 24 hours a day, so that disrupted some of my families' lives as well as one of my Reiki friends. I'm so thankful for my caregivers. The stem cell transplant was much harder on my body. I did get sick, I lost my hair, and afterward, my immune system was shot.

At the end of the month, we did tests again, and my doctor was very happy. He said, "I've only seen this once before." "You should go home, have a glass of wine, and celebrate; we can't find any trace of cancer." But in his next breath, he says, "But don't be fooled, it's still there."

You may be wondering where the divine timing comes into play. Well, if I hadn't learned about Reiki or the other forms of energy healing, I believe I would've had a more predictable outcome, rather than one where I'm one out of two, who came out of all the treatments, not showing any sign of Multiple Myeloma and all within six months. Without Divine timing, I wouldn't have met all these amazing healers I can now call my friends. Before my very first chemo session, my friend Nancy gave me an Energy Healing session. I continued to do self-healing, along with some shamanic journeys to enhance the western medicine I was receiving. When it came time for my stem cell transplant, my friend Laudie came to the hospital to give me a Reiki session, and she also stayed with me at the Hope Lodge for a week to provide support and more Reiki sessions. My friends were sending me healings, which can easily be done remotely. I cut out all alcohol, chocolate, sugar, and I consumed what I was craving, grapefruit. Grapefruit is full of vitamin C and has been shown to help with cancer treatments.

Being attuned to energy healing, you are more aware of what your body wants, and you notice changes when and if you listen, or even when you don't listen, your body will speak to you. When I first had signs I was getting sick, I ignored them. I felt too healthy for there to be something really wrong with me. This could also be that stubborn side of me. When I was faced with that nasty C-word, I didn't panic. I always felt I would overcome whatever I was dealt. I had support and love from my family and friends. My husband had to help me in ways he never had to before, and I had to learn to let him. Accepting help is one of the big lessons for me. Here I am over five years later, and I am thriving, not just surviving.

This experience was all part of my soul journey. By sharing these words, I'm bringing you along on my journey. I believe lessons are learned and then need to be shared with others. By going through these experiences, we have more compassion for those who need us, and we inspire those around us.

## The Tool

We are all made of energy. Everything is made of energy. The difference is the frequency at which that energy exists.

Reiki is a Japanese form of Energy Healing that has been around for almost 100 years. Just like most other forms of Energy Healing, the healing source comes from the Universe or God. It flows through the top of your head, the crown chakra, through you and out your hands. You can call in this healing energy simply by rubbing your hands together or tapping on your thymus, which is located on your chest.

The purpose of Reiki, just like other energy healing modalities, is to move or shift the energy within the body, to clear blockages, to relax the body, to reduce stress, all for the purpose of giving your body the chance to heal itself. Our bodies are designed to heal themselves. They're always creating new cells; healing cuts and bruises, bones, and wounds. Shifting the energy gives your body that extra boost it sometimes needs for the big stuff. It also helps with emotional and mental issues.

We have many energy centers in our body, which are called Chakras. Chakras can be described as spinning pools of energy associated with certain organs within the body. I had just mentioned the crown chakra above, which is at the top of your head. It's one of the seven main chakras in the body, but there are several others in and outside your physical body.

If the energy in your body is flowing smoothly, the chakras are spinning and doing their job of keeping your body healthy. You also have an energy body located outside of your body. Many call this your aura. The aura has seven layers of energy, each layer having a specific task. So you can see the body we live in is quite complex. But it's also quite simple. By helping to reduce stress in your life, eat a proper diet, and regularly working to clear your chakras and all other energy centers in your body, you could live a long healthy life.

Any time you experience a trauma, have an argument with someone, or probably even more damaging, when you don't speak your mind and hold your frustrations in, you could be causing your body to create an energy block. That lower vibrational energy collects in your body or aura and can eventually make you sick if you don't move it out. There are simple techniques you can do to help move this energy. Breathing is one of the easiest. I'm not talking about the unconscious breathing we do all the time to stay alive, but a conscious breath, deep breathing, consciously moving energy through your body with the intention to clear out unwanted energy and bringing in good energy.

Using the following exercises, you'll be given a chance to start releasing some of the energy blocks you may have. You begin to feel lighter, more energetic, sleep better, feel less stressed, and more balanced.

## The Exercises

Breath is one of the easiest ways to shift your energy. You can focus on what you want to breathe into your body and breathe out what you want to release. There are many breathing techniques; this is one that I like to use. I call it the Apple Breathing Technique. It's used to move the breath up and down your central channel, aka your spine. It helps to clear your main chakras and keeps the energy flowing in both directions.

## THE APPLE BREATHING TECHNIQUE

In a sitting position, imagine that your spine is the core of an apple, and there is a big red apple surrounding your body. Then as you take a breath in, imagine the breath is coming up from the earth through your tailbone or root chakra. Bring this breath into your belly, and as you exhale, bring the breath up your spine and out the top of your head. As the breath leaves your body, imagine the breath going up to the Divine and then comes back down around the outside of the apple, back into the earth, as you breathe in capturing the earths energy. It then circulates, back up through your root chakra into your belly. Repeat this at least three times and then switch directions. Start with an incoming breath coming in through the crown chakra at the top of your head, down your spine, into the belly. Exhale the breath out the root chakra into the earth. The breath then circulates around the outside of the apple, up to the Divine, capture that heavenly energy, and bring it down into your crown chakra as you take another deep breath in, down the spine, and into the belly. Again, repeat this direction at least three times.

I mentioned previously that I would do self-healing at times. This is a simple technique that anyone can do.

## SELF-HEALING

Take a couple of deep breaths to calm yourself. Rub your hands together to stir up some energy. Place one hand on your chest, the Heart Chakra, and the other hand in the stomach area, above the belly button. This is the Solar Plexus Chakra. Breathe in the energy coming from your hands. Breathe out what you want to release. Hold your hands there as long as it feels comfortable. When you are ready, simply release your hands and sense the calmness within your body.

Our bodies are designed with several energy systems. One is called the Meridian System. Energy moves along these meridians throughout our body, keeping our bodies and organs healthy. The Triple Warmer Meridian is designed to trigger our Fight or Flight response in the case of an emergency. It was designed to give us a temporary boost of energy to help us flee danger. In today's world, our fight or flight response is active most of the time due to our stressful lives, and that isn't the way our bodies were meant to be. By reversing the Triple Warmer Meridian, we're helping our bodies to relax, to release cortisol, to give our bodies a chance to heal. Try this Triple Warmer Meridian reversal process to help reduce stress.

## TRIPLE WARMER MERIDIAN REVERSAL

Using your fingertips, you will be tracing the Triple Warmer Meridian in the reverse direction to soothe the Triple Warmer Meridian. This meridian starts at the tip of your ring finger, flows up your arm, over your shoulder, and the side of your neck. It then traces around the outside of your ear and ends at your temple. Since we are soothing this meridian, you'll be tracing it backward, starting at the temple.

Cross your right arm in front of you; place your fingertips on your left temple. Take a deep breath in and as you exhale, in a smooth motion, move your hand up, over and around the back of your left ear, ending by your earlobe. This is like making a half-circle around your ear. Continue to bring your right hand down the left side of your neck, over your shoulder towards your left arm. Then proceed to bring your right hand down the outside of your left arm, over your hand, exiting over your ring finger. Repeat this three times and then switch to the other side with your left hand starting at your right temple.

I hope you found these exercises fun and easy to do. For a video of these exercises and more, please go to:
pambohlken.com/resources.

Because of her vast array of life experiences, Pam Bohlken is able to bring compassion and her joy of helping others into each Energy Healing session. Using Reiki or Vibrational Sound Therapy (VST) she helps her clients to release stress, to help their bodies relax to a point where they have the ability to heal themselves. Reiki is a hands-on healing method, and Vibrational Sound Therapy brings in the soothing sounds and vibration of singing bowls while being placed on the body.

Pam is also certified in the Marisa Peer method of Rapid Transformational Therapy (RTT) using hypnosis to help her clients discover deep-seeded beliefs that are currently causing emotional or health issues. Sessions are available in person or virtually.

Pam regularly performs Sound Meditations, using her beautiful Himalayan Singing Bowls to bring the soothing rhythmic tones into group sessions.

Pam lives in rural Wisconsin with her husband, where she can enjoy being in nature. She is an amateur herbalist, and she loves spending time with her grandchildren, gardening, and sewing. To learn more about Pam, contact her, or find current online and in-person events, go to pambohlken.com

# CHAPTER 15

# Mindset Mastery
## Recognizing Accomplishments for Radical Self-Care

### BY KIM B MILLER

## My Story

### Haiku
How many times do
you have to fall before you
stop tripping yourself?

As a spoken word poet, I've performed in several states. I performed on stages I would have never imagined possible. I write poetry almost every day, and when I use my poetic voice, I touch people. The response I receive from a live audience is a thing of beauty. Still, with all that success, I realized I still didn't think I was doing enough. I was always trying to write more, perform more, and get hired more. I didn't take the time to "survey my own backyard." You know us poets cannot talk in simple terms, right? What I mean is, I didn't take time to see what I already accomplished. I was so busy trying to do more, I didn't take time to enjoy, embrace, and celebrate what I already did. I would say to myself: *You have not done enough*. To make matters worse, I didn't use anything to track the milestones that I completed. I had no physical list of my successful planning, and I looked at completion as success. It didn't matter if I wrote another chapter of my book, it wasn't complete, and it wasn't published, so it was not something I would consider successful. I had to learn incremental success. I should warn you; poets are wordy.

Incremental success is acknowledging each step done before a project is completed. When I was working on a project, I ignored the planning, steps and energy I used to complete individual milestones. I would only label a goal a success once I completed everything. That was me. I could not see I was limiting myself. I really thought I had not done much. I would look at other poets and assume they had done more or were doing more. The push to be greater in my eyes was a real desire. I know some of you are thinking what's wrong with trying to be greater. There's nothing wrong with trying to be greater if you know your starting point and recognize your growth. At that time, I did neither of those things. I just kept pushing myself to do more.

### Haiku

True fact: if you lis-
ten to a lie long enough,
it becomes your truth.

Even when I was complimented about how much I'd done, in my mind, I negated the compliment. Don't get me wrong, I appreciated their opinion, but I was astounded when people would say how well I was doing. It wasn't until I upgraded and revamped my website that I started to "see me." On the new site, I posted most of my past events. I included magazines and books that published my haiku. I took a look, sat back, and embraced my work. I really loved what I did. So, I celebrated myself and looked at how my mindset was limiting me. I knew I needed to change. I had to make my victories known to me. I had to learn to acknowledge the preparation, plans, and steps. I opened myself to a new perspective. I made a radical change, and the results have been astounding. I keep my "to-do it list" full. When I accomplish anything on my list, it is "conquer time." No more mini checkmarks. I make purple stars on each thing that I do. I accentuate my incremental steps with appreciation. Every link in my chain to success is needed and honored.

My music playlist is full of powerful anthems that speak to me. I play music to make my vision more vivid. I am bold now, and my love for truth is watered every day. Yes, I planted a seed in my own garden called "knowledge of self." Now it is my favorite plant.

What happened with my poetry and focus as a result? I branched out into different areas of poetry. I tried something new. Before I sharpened my conquering skills, I stayed complacent. Now, I add things to my list with determination. I'll give you an example. When I first heard a form of poetry called haiku, I thought: *I wonder if I can make powerful poems in 17 syllables.* Now, I write them almost daily. Why am I talking about haiku? Well, most people don't know I was not even going to try to write haiku. They seemed confining at first. I could write freely and not have to be concerned with structure, lines, and syllable counts. I ultimately decided to make time on my "power list" (to-do list) to encapsulate a poem into seventeen syllables, and now I am known for my haiku. I'm an award-winning poet because of my haiku. I learned to grow, blossom, and conquer when I learned to define, see, and celebrate my victories.

I want you to rebuild your whole recognition process, so you can gravitate toward unapologetic pride in your victories and rampant celebrations for your accomplishments.

### Haiku
Please recognize your
accomplishments or you will
label them failures.

## The Tool

Here are the steps to go from dreaming about doing things to radial concrete growth.

First, find music that inspires you. I suggest that you start off with ten songs. Music that changes your mood. Pick several songs that move you mentally. They can be songs with victorious themes or songs that make you smile. You will be rotating songs so they are not repetitive. Write down your first 10 song titles:

1. _____

2. _____

3. _____

4. _____

5. _____

6. _____

7. _____

8. _____

9. _____

10. _____

Now you have this radical list of music that moves you, it's time to actually play those songs because you are going translate your goals into an obtainable list.

Second, get a notebook, if you are a "paper person" and label the notebook something spectacular. If you are a "computer person," you can type it in as well. Just make sure you name the file something magnificent. I want you to look at that notebook or file and beam with pride.

Now add an actual list of things you want to get accomplished each day or week. This is an important step that people often overlook because they think they will remember everything. Here's the problem with that train of thought: first, you will forget the steps if they are not written down. Second, when it is time to recognize what you completed, you will overlook the things you accomplished. People tend to judge themselves harshly. So, if you ask yourself what you have achieved, generally you will say nothing even if you have done a lot. Why is that? Well, people tend to look at completion as a victory. In other words, when everything is complete, then they label it a victory. Don't overlook the fact that victory arises from completing steps too. You don't even realize you are categorizing your success in such a narrow way until you take steps to actually evaluate your progress. I want you to stop congratulating yourself only at the completion of a task and start applauding your incremental accomplishments as well.

Keep in mind; your goal is to take your dreams and breathe life into them. Take the ideological wonderment out and put concrete steps in place. Now that your goals are "getting real," don't talk yourself out of greatness just because it actually involves some planning.

This is very important, so please understand your to-do list is adjustable. Life happens, and you don't want to be so stern with your list that you don't allow for spontaneous moments and unforeseen complications.

So let's go. Write down your daily or weekly bold goals. Keep this Kim-ism (saying) in mind as you write: your Lamborghini mentality won't help you if you only have Ford goals. In other words, make sure your effort and your goals are on equal footing. If you have big goals, make sure your effort matches what you are trying to accomplish. There's no point in having a grandiose mentality toward your to-do list if you only wrote non-challenging tasks. Stretch outside of your comfort zone.

Alright back to your list, take your "destiny" and break it into individual successful steps. This is the time to be realistic and not overzealous. Make it achievable. Don't sabotage yourself with a timeline you know is impossible to keep. Always leave some time open and available each day. Your to-do list should not be so confining that it becomes something to avoid. You can use a timeframe like (between 12-2) if you find it helpful. Keep in mind, creativity waits for no one, and you don't want to cut it off simply because the time you allotted has ended. Be flexible and let your "genius faucet" run.

Now you have your "power" list (previously known as your to-do list) call it something radical. It is not a to-do list. "Yawn, that's boring." Think of something inspiring like: "I Got Open Road," "I'm So Dope," "Let's Do This," "On My Way to Victory," "Stepping to Greatness." You get the point, use your imagination.

Next, you are going to research three people and/or companies who are successful. You are trying to find failures they were vulnerable enough to admit to. Everyone has failed. They are successful because they learned from their mistakes and persevered. They did not eliminate mistakes. They learned. One of my go-to stories is the one for the cleaner 409. It is on their website. I had no idea they failed 408 times. It's a fascinating story. You never know where you will find inspiration. List the three you researched here:

1. _____

2. _____

3. _____

Keep this information bookmarked on your computer or print the details, and put it with your "power" list. You may need it later.

Now that you have done some research, the smooth path you thought those famous people had was not so simple, after all. We tend to make assumptions about what success looks like. Use their experiences as a learning tool. Remember, success is not a competition with anyone else. You are not trying to outdo anyone. You are trying to be the best you can be. Don't use your growth to show anyone that they were wrong about you. Use your success to show yourself you were right about you. Focus on this Kimism (saying): dreams don't need cosigners. Be you, do you, for you!

### Haiku
Be who you are not
to impress but to inspire.
Let your greatness drip.

What should you do when you don't accomplish everything on your "power" list? First, don't default back to your old mentality of "I'm a failure." Don't let a misstep turn you against your progress. Second, evaluate what took place. Learn from it. Rewrite the step and keep pushing forward. You don't need to give up. You are not going to stop working on your dreams because of mistakes, rejection, or uncertainty. Keep walking boldly in your purpose.

Now you have your "I got this" playlist. You listened to your "power" music while you renamed your notebook and wrote (or typed) your "radical ain't ordinary" list of things you are going to demolish. You are ready. Pick a day to check on your progress, like every Friday at 7, and make it "a whole mood." Rock that playlist and check on your accomplishments. When you accomplish something, don't just check it off. Write something innovative like: crushed it, demolished it, pure joy, nothing but net, creativity won or I did that!

If you were not effective at a task, write revamp or redo next to it. Take time to evaluate what went wrong and right, then write up a new step and add it back to your "power" list and proceed. Give yourself permission to be human, but don't be destructive. Don't rehash everything you have ever done wrong. This one step needs to be addressed, not you. You are not the problem, but you have the solution. Read that again and own that truth. If you are feeling down, look at the successful people you already researched. They had missteps and kept going. Read about another one, get invigorated, and keep rocking that "power" list.

### Haiku
You got your own mind
twisted. You don't realize
that you are gifted.

Why bother with the inspirational music and the "power" list? What's the point? The point is to reboot your mindset about your vision. Some of you didn't realize you were setting yourself up for and expecting failure because of your mindset. Some of you were making goals that were important to other people, but honestly, they were not your goals. Some even relied on other people to make their dreams relevant or worthy. You don't need their validation of your dreams. Change your vision and challenge your mindset so you can identify who you really are.

### Haiku
You were looking for
someone powerful. I just
showed you your mirror.

Once you change the environment in which you write your goals, you change. That change, along with the way you acknowledge your incremental accomplishments will have you making "power" moves. Music is a great motivator. Use it to build momentum. Mindset changes will lead you to radical moves. Go ahead with your powerful self, and don't let fear hold you back.

### Haiku
It's okay to be
scared. Do it anyway. Scared
people succeed too.

Now that you are working on your "power" list, you can go directly to my website for some complementary information. I will also let you take a look at my "musical victory" playlist. Of course, you'll have more haiku and Kimisms to enjoy.

Use the link listed below because only the people who've read this book will know this page exists. I will not include it on the website's menu. I want this page to be exclusive to you conquerors. http://www.kimbmiller.com/chapter15

Kim is a native New Yorker, born in Brooklyn, New York.

She's an empowering motivational speaker that touches your heart, mind, and soul.

This spoken word poet loves writing and performing. Her poetry is her heart expressed in words: opinionated, blunt, thought-provoking, and real.

She has been the featured poet/speaker/facilitator at events in several states: NY, MD, DC, VA, SC, PA, CA, CO, NC. She also performed at The National Black Theater in New York, and she was the featured poet at the Atlas Performing Arts Center in DC. She facilitated a haiku class in Denver, Colorado (a National Poetry event).

Kim is the author of several poetry books, and she recently released a journal.

She is the 2019 Southern Fried Poetry Haiku Champion, and 2018 Black Poetry Café Put Your Money Where Your Mouth Is slam champion.

She mentors students and poets on writing and performing poetry. She believes in building young minds to accomplish great things.

Kim started her t-shirt line in 2018, which features her haiku and sayings.

Kim believes thinking is her oxygen, and words are her blood.

# CHAPTER 16

# Angel Energy
## Basking in Angel Energy as a Healing Practice

### BY LILIA SHOSHANNA RAE

## My Story

I was crouching in the corner of our dining room. My arms were wrapped around my shins in what was like a vertical fetal position. I was desperately seeking some sense of safety from the two walls forming that corner. He could only get at one side of me if he chose to come after me, which I knew he would before too long. I only had a moment of respite, a moment to plead with God, "Help me. I don't know what to do. I don't know where to go. I'm so afraid. I need to leave, but I'm scared that if I leave, he will find me, and then things will be even worse. How did this happen to me? What am I to do?"

I felt helpless. Hope had disappeared into six months of daily hell with my then-husband interrogating me each day, "Where did you go at lunch? Who did you talk to? Why did it take you so long to get home? Who did you see? I saw you look at that man across the street. Are you having an affair with him? What about that guy at work? Did you talk to him? Is there another guy? Who did you see in your office today? Were you alone with him?" After about 30 questions, as I tried to tell him through tears and frantically growing fears that nothing was going on, he would quiet down and let me finish making dinner for him and our two young children. My son was seven. My daughter was three. They were usually in the other room playing during these onslaughts of interrogation, but I knew they could hear his raised voice and my begging for him to stop and my desperate pleas for him to believe me.

Six months. Every day. Every morning before work. Every evening after work. I felt I was losing my mind—certainly, I had lost any hope that things would change. Yet I could not lose my children. I had to do what I could to hang on for them. He wasn't hurting them, but he threatened to take them. And he was from a country that had no diplomatic relations with the US. If he took them, I might never see them again.

I don't tell this story very often. It's hard for me to write about even now. It was hell. Yet by some miracle, I survived it, and my children, including the one in my belly at the time, and I, turned our lives around to not only survive but thrive. We have so many blessings in our lives now. I am so grateful.

When I look back on this time, I recognize that I had angels around me, protecting me, but I didn't know that then. It would take another ten years before angels would break through to my conscious awareness and let me know that they're around us—that they didn't get stuck in the pages of the Bible. They're available and accessible to each of us, whether we are aware of them or not. We need only ask for their assistance for us to receive their bounteous gifts of inspiration, guidance, and healing. We don't even have to see or hear them to receive their gifts. They use whatever will get our attention to give us signs and clues—feathers in unexpected places, repeating numbers on digital clocks, even books jumping off shelves.

Once angels revealed themselves to me, my life changed in so many ways. I found my spiritual path, I left my job as a lawyer for the state legislature, and I grew into my role as Angel Connector, helping people connect to their personal angel team so that they can more easily and successfully accomplish their reason for coming into this lifetime—their soul's purpose or life mission.

My angels tell me that helping us live our soul's purpose is their main focus. While they will help us with mundane tasks like finding a parking spot or remembering where we put our keys, that kind of assistance is intended to help us build a relationship with them, so we trust the more important guidance we receive from them. They prefer helping us identify and share our unique gifts as we live a life on purpose.

Shortly after angels made themselves known to me, they shared with me what they believe is my mission in life—one so huge it has taken decades to understand what it means for me and just how I'm to accomplish it. I have resisted it, denied it, felt too small for it, seemed unworthy of it, and struggled to describe it to others. Basically, I have had to grow into it, evolve so that I could accept it, and release my blocks around it so I could help others claim their mission.

What is calling you? What feels so huge that you don't feel worthy or capable, and yet it won't leave you alone? What shows up in your dreams, in your vision boards, and in the restlessness of your heart?

Whatever it is, your personal angel team can help you remove any blocks in your way—whether it is a lack of material resources or hindering internal messaging, angels can help you move beyond the obstacles so that you can achieve what only you can do—those things you were born into this life to share with the world. By doing so, you'll not only help those you serve, but you'll see amazing shifts in your life.

It's more important now than ever that each of us claims and shares our gifts fully. The world is hurting. Many are living a life that feels like hell—or witnessing hellish attacks on others.

Globally, we are seeing the abuse of humans, abuse of natural resources, climate change, earthquakes, volcanic eruptions, and violent storms. Then on top of everything, we have a tiny little virus wreaking havoc as it defies detection until someone starts coughing and has so much trouble breathing, they are put on a ventilator.

The world needs each of us to step into our gifts and share our uniqueness and our passions. Angels want to help us do that.

As for my huge mission, it's called "bringing heaven on earth." No small order, eh? Those are the exact words I heard during a workshop on spiritual gifts and soul's purpose. We were led into a meditation with the central question, what is your purpose in life? I heard those words, and I wanted to pretend I didn't hear them. They seemed crazy to me—way too huge and pretentious. Yet when the facilitator asked us to share what we received in our meditation, I spoke them because I couldn't deny what I heard.

Bringing heaven on earth? What does that mean? How does one do that? Well, I certainly knew what hell was, and I didn't want to ever experience that again.

As a society, we are facing a whole lot of hellishness. The only way through it is to begin with ourselves, to find the qualities of heaven within, and then to share them with the world. That is why each of us tapping into our unique gifts is so important. Not only do the gifts themselves hold the qualities of heaven, but as we share them, we feel joy, peace, deep fulfillment, a sense of abundance and prosperity no matter what the financial impact is. We feel the flow of life. We feel whole.

Wholeness. That can feel a bit like heaven, too. It reminds me of a message I gave recently with the guidance of my angels. I do a Facebook Live once a week based on a topic my angels suggest to me. They give me inspiration and specific words to weave into what I already know about the topic. This particular day, the topic was wholeness. Midway through the Live, the word "holiness" came to me, and, as it did, it touched a funny bone inside. I started to giggle—right there on Facebook Live. As I giggled, I realized I was feeling joy in the moment, and when I feel joy, it's as if I have little bubbles of energy floating up inside, in a kind of celebration, reminding me of champagne or a spritzer. Light, airy, and joyful. I have come to know this as the core of my "work," my passion and purpose. To find ways to that sense of wholeness within that connects me to a sense of holiness, a spaciousness in which joy can bubble up spontaneously and freely.

When we can learn to do that no matter what is going on in our external world, we are bringing a little slice of heaven into the world. We may find it's the starting point for us, the foundation from which we can bring whatever else we are called to bring. Or it may be enough because we will impact the person in front of us, and that will impact the next, and the waves of heavenly energy will ripple out.

So, I invite you to experiment with me. Whether you have ever connected to angel energy or not, imagine that they would delight in helping you tap into your wholeness, your holiness, your heaven inside of you. The tool I describe below can help with that because I show you how to lean into their energy and just bask—just as you might lean back on a sandy beach and bask in the sunshine. It is that easy.

## The Tool

Basking in angel energy is something anyone can do, whether they ever have had an experience with an angel or not. You can use your imagination, and it will have the same effect as if you can feel, see, or hear with your senses.

Begin by finding a quiet place where you'll be undisturbed for 30 minutes or more. Sit comfortably as you would for a meditation or contemplation practice. Close your eyes and notice your breath.

Allow the awareness of your breath to bring you into the present moment. Notice how your body is moving with each breath. Notice what you're feeling with each breath. If you find your mind begins to engage in thought, kindly say to your mind, "thank you, but not now."

Return your awareness to your breath. Once you feel deeply present to the moment, take your awareness to your feet and pause for a moment, sensing your feet and their connection to the floor beneath them. The soles of your feet connect your soul to the earth. Take a moment to feel gratitude for all you've received from this beautiful planet that provides all you need for your nurturance and survival in your body. Allow that gratitude to strengthen your connection to our beautiful planet. Allow the connection to ground your energy so that you can become even more present to this moment and even more open to receiving the blessing of energy from the angelic realm.

With even more gratitude, allow your awareness to travel up your inner core, bringing the grounding energy from the earth into your whole body, through your heart space and up to the top of your head and pause. Then as if you had eyes on the top of your head, visualize all that is above you. Perhaps first it's a ceiling and a roof beyond that sky. Acknowledge that there's so much more beyond what you can see or even imagine. Give thanks for this sense of expansiveness that's all part of the creation in which you're living. Continuing with a deep sense of gratitude, bring your awareness back down to your heart space and pause. Feel the mixture of grounding energy from planet earth and expansive energies for all that is beyond our knowing.

All of this is preparation for you to open to the loving and nurturing energy of the angelic realm. Angels are always available and accessible to us. They do not require us to prepare for their assistance, and yet we benefit more when we do. They do ask us to invite them into our lives because they respect our free will. So in this moment, set an intention for what you would like to receive in this moment—perhaps you merely want to feel more relaxed, perhaps there is something physical that you would like to bring some healing energy to, perhaps an issue in your life that you could use some inspiration or guidance—especially on how you can more easily bring your unique gifts to the world. Whatever you wish to receive assistance with, bring it to mind and set it as an intention.

Now let that go and give permission for your angel team to assist you. Your angel team includes your guardian angel and any other angels who your soul is calling forward for only your highest good, to connect and be with you in this moment. You don't need to know them by name. You don't need to be able to feel or see them. Merely trust they're there to serve you for your highest good.

Relax into the moment. Allow yourself to just be. You may be able to feel a sense of loving energy surrounding you. If so, relax into it. Allow yourself to be held by it. If you catch yourself thinking or analyzing, kindly tell your mind once more, "thank you, but not now," and drop back into your heart space that has been so carefully prepared to receive the blessings of your angels in this moment, here and now. Relax into this moment. Bask in it. This is basking in angel energy, and it can be anything you want it to be. You may feel you're being bathed in love and light. You may be given a visual that holds a special meaning to you. You may see an angel or a whole host of angels. You may hear a word or two. Just relax into whatever this moment is for you.

At some point, it will feel complete. You can begin to bring your awareness to your room and to your body. Bring it back slowly and gently so you can retain as much of this loving energy in your body as possible. Allow it to continue to bathe your cells and organs with its loving, nurturing energy.

And give thanks to all of those beautiful angels who were with you, who want you to know they're always available and accessible to you. You need only ask.

You may want to journal your experience. If you received a message or a visual be sure to write it down. It may hold even more meaning for you as you reflect on it. Whatever you experienced, write it down.

Like any spiritual practice, basking in angel energy can become more effective with repetition. Set an intention to do this every day until you feel you can do it with ease whenever you feel the need.

Some find it easier to use a recorded meditation to guide them. Check out the recorded meditation I've prepared for you at this link: https://www.liliashoshannarae.com/free-meditation.

After thirty years as a state legislative lawyer, Lilia Shoshanna Rae decided she could no longer postpone her passion as a messenger for the angelic realm to help create heaven on earth. In her book, *The Art of Listening to Angels,* she shares her story of how angels entered her life and helped her transform it by opening to their wisdom and love. She shares the five-step process they gave her to develop the art of listening to angels.

Lilia now helps lightworkers and spiritual healers access angel wisdom and love through Angel Connection sessions that empower clients to develop their own angel connections and receive support as they bring forth their unique gifts and talents on their spiritual path.

Since 2003, Lilia has been a Usui and Karuna® Reiki Master and a teacher of the sacred mysteries of alchemy, sacred geometry, and the Enneagram. She has a unique talent for leading meditations to help clients attain deep states of peace and access inner wisdom.

Lilia is a contributing author in several Amazon bestselling anthologies. In the first edition of *Pebbles in the Pond: Transforming the World One Person at a Time,* her chapter "Life Is a Hoot If We'd Only Laugh," gives the reader three tools for continuing their transformational practice, including the gift of laughter. Her chapter in *Pebbles in the Pond (Wave Five)* entitled "The Time Is Now: Are You Ready?" shares guidance for all of us to be who we came here to be and do what we came here to do.

Responding to the call of one of her dearest friends, Lilia was a founding member of a nonprofit in the Annapolis, MD, area called A Community of Transformation (ACT), whose vision is to be an inspirational, heart-centered community that nurtures profound transformation. Serving on its board since 2003, she was also a contributing author in a bestselling anthology, *Circular Leadership: Together We Rise,* that describes a new model for leadership based on the experiences of ACT.

Lilia serves as a prayer chaplain and facilitates church services as a platform assistant at Unity by the Bay in Annapolis, where she has felt nurtured and supported on her spiritual path.

One of Lilia's core beliefs is that when we live on purpose, we bring heaven on earth, her personal mission, and "possible" dream. Check out her blogs at https://www.liliashoshannarae.com/blog. And be sure to check out her meditation to help you bask in amazing angel energy at https://www.liliashoshannarae.com/free-meditation.

# CHAPTER 17

# Visioning
## Put Yourself in the Driver's Seat of Your Life

### BY LIZ GOLL LERNER, LCPAT, LPC, ATR-BC

The night before I began writing this chapter, I had a dream. A lioness, bathed in sunlight, lounged on the red couch in front of the living room window of my first marital home.

The room was flooded with glimmering light that extended all the way to the back garden, showcasing her golden fur. She was strong and majestic yet soft, approachable.

Suddenly from the back garden entered the lion. Massive mane and a broad golden-brown body, he exuded strength and flexibility without aggression.

I thought, *Oh my! We have lions!* And a feeling of great awe and joy came over me.

It's no surprise to me that these beings showed up in my dream. Not only do they represent the balance of feminine and masculine energy–which we all use to keep us simultaneously inwardly and outwardly directed–but these lions have the characteristics of a healthy Protector.

Strong, flexible, benevolent, strategic, observant.

The Protector is an archetype I discovered operating in my life over the years, sometimes acting as a saboteur, protecting me in ways that prevented me from seeing important truths. Sometimes, acting as a champion by helping me actualize my dreams.

Through my work as a coach and therapist, I developed a model based on the 12 amazing archetypes I had come to understand were always at work within us. Essentially creating our inner operating system whether we're aware of them or not.

What I knew was that each archetype has the power to sabotage us, and each has the power to champion us. It's only when we are conscious of them, get to know them inside and out, and become adept at activating the archetype we need in any specific moment, through what I call our Central Core Self, that we can leverage their power and strengths to our advantage.

Of course, each of the 12 archetypes has a unique role, and the Protector, when healthy and acting as our champion, is key to manifesting our vision and creating new and positive outcomes in our life–especially when we find ourselves in the type of challenging situations that trigger our Protector to show up.

Enter the lions from my dream...steadfastly by my side as I write this chapter.

Here is the story of how my Protector helped me discover one of the most important truths of my life and how, by understanding that truth, I was able to transform it from the unconscious saboteur it once was, to a part of myself I can draw strength from at will.

During my now-defunct 23-year marriage, my Protector acted as my saboteur a lot of the time. As in any relationship, my partner and I had many tough decisions to make, and my Protector was involved in every one of them.

That meant my entire history was involved:

What I had learned about responding to conflict or joy growing up; everything I had gleaned from my previous relationships; what I had discovered while counseling my clients; and, of course, all my hopes, dreams, and beliefs. In short, all of my past experiences and learning affected how my Protector presented itself.

My husband and I had a complicated relationship from the beginning. Red Flag? Yes.

But I wanted it to work. And, if I'm completely honest, I believed that people could change, that is, if they really want to...and, of course, there's the rub!

Suffice it to say, I made many not-so-accurate assumptions when it came to choosing my life partner. I also had an agenda.

I was 33. I wanted to be married, and I thought I had found the right man. My Protector's voice was in my ear, telling me *If I don't get married now, I probably never will!* An unrealistic fear for certain, but my Protector's job was to protect and support me, whether or not the fear was based in truth or an unsubstantiated belief.

At this point in my life, I was also focused on spirituality—creating a better me and a better world. It's still a primary focus, but at the time, it translated into: *Why not work on myself to make my relationship better?* Another red flag!

After all, it's one thing to evolve for yourself and quite another to try to change one's authentic nature to make someone else happy. Yet I found myself thinking, *so what if there are a few issues, we'll work them out!*

The Protector was both saboteur and champion at that moment because it was helping me follow what I believed I wanted, but it was using misguided information I was unknowingly providing.

Regardless, I still held a vision about the possibility of our relationship. We both must have wanted it because we worked at it for a long time. The problem was that success meant each of us would need to change—a difficult proposition, to say the least.

During that time, my Protector kept me safe by fighting the good fight to help me stay intact while navigating a difficult relationship because I wanted it and myself to flourish. Unfortunately, those things were at odds.

As I write this now my heart hurts thinking about how I let so many moments that felt disrespectful to me go. I even had parental voices weighing in with advice to keep at it. If there were nothing positive, I would have left. But so many people's agendas, along with my desire not to let my marriage "fail," made me second guess myself.

As a result, my Protector went into overdrive to make it possible for me to stay. But, in truth, I wasn't trusting my own heart.

We did succeed in many ways and had an amazing, beautiful baby boy. Even though it didn't help our marriage, my former husband and I still agree that having our son was the best decision we ever made. Yet by the time our son was two, we were in couples' therapy, and I remember the shock I felt in one early session:

*Oh my god, we're living in two different universes. My partner's experiences and perspectives about everything we ever did or said are completely different than mine! What am I going to do now?!*

It was later that week while at a friend's house that my husband said something about me that was meant to be funny. It triggered everything I felt in the counselor's office. I sobbed to my friend incredulously, "I can't believe I just wasted the last eight years of my life!" *All that work for nothing!*

Wake up call!"

My Protector went into overdrive again. I had decisions to make, and I was scared. I had a beautiful toddler, but now what?

I had given up most of my work to be a stay-at-home mom. I knew my best option was to move out of state near family. But I also knew I would never take my son away from his father. We were older parents, and we wanted our son to have both of us, and we each wanted the joy of raising him.

I realized clarity was what I needed. I could not act unconsciously. My life and my baby's happiness were all that mattered. What I needed was my Protector to operate as my champion.

I knew it hadn't meant to sabotage me previously. I was aware from all my personal and professional work that I was the guide, the one in charge. Although I thought I knew what I was doing before, I was fairly unconscious during that challenging time, and I had chosen to ignore some of my real motivations and fears.

No matter how aware we are of the various aspects of ourselves, or how much personal growth work we do, or how self-aware we are most of the time, we all still fall prey to losing our clarity at times, acting from our unconscious or simply ignoring the signs.

So, at that point in my life, all my Protector could do was follow me. And it did.

Until I woke up.

Getting clear again changed everything. I accepted that my partner and I would never reach our potential as a couple. I decided to stay, shifted my focus to remain a family, and navigated our relationship from a place of strength and purpose.

That was my new vision. One I was able to choose with full self-awareness, honesty, and certainty. It was what my best self wanted at the time, and while it may not have been the right decision for someone else, it was for me.

Of course, there were many ups and downs. Lots of visits to our counselor. Often, I needed to re-visit that choice and re-commit to my vision, but I was able to do it from a place of clear-headedness and calm. I wasn't fooling myself anymore.

Our vision was to have a healthy son, and that's exactly what we got.

Now, that doesn't mean my partner and I solved all our problems or didn't have to deal with new ones. It also doesn't mean it didn't take significant energy to keep the status quo during that time. But what I gained was an even deeper knowledge of the strength of visioning with a clear purpose.

We were going to uncouple, no question. We simply consciously chose to wait for the healthiest moment for our son.

The day I knew it was time to end the relationship, I also recognized I would need a new purpose-driven vision. One I could communicate with clarity, and that would allow all three of us to prepare.

My new vision was to reformulate our family, not destroy it.

To accomplish that, I needed my Protector actively awake, aware, and conscious. Specifically, to support my plan for getting everyone on the same page in a wise and above-board way. I believed that family and couples' therapy would be the best choice for preparing us and would also give my son a voice. All agreed.

It wasn't always smooth sailing, though. I found myself getting irritated quite often and sucked into the same old fights. I saw that I had fallen back on my automatic responses to conflict, and I had to stop that from happening.

Becoming conscious of it was, again, the key. Suddenly I realized that every time I didn't get sucked in, chose not to make a comment or handled a situation from a neutral place, the negative interchange didn't occur.

Over time we began to deal with each other differently. It took huge amounts of self-control and lots of missteps, but it worked. Because I detached from the hurt and focused on my bigger vision, my Protector helped me react differently.

There were no more battles, but not because I was giving in to someone else or giving up to avoid being hurt. It was because I was true to myself–to my vision.

By the time we decided to pull the plug, everything was settled in three weeks.

The move-out organized. A separation party planned. And my doorway into a new life opened, my Protector, holding the door.

The ability to activate the champion aspect of your Protector is a tool I want you to have. In your most challenging and vital moments, your Protector–as this archetype's name suggests–will quite literally help you save the day. Be the lions at your side.

## The Tool: Put Yourself in the Driver's Seat of Your Life

### PART ONE: Transforming Your Protector from Saboteur to Champion

To start, create time and space for yourself. You'll need about 30 minutes to an hour for this process, and finding a private, comfortable spot–whether inside or outside–will support you in doing this inner work. I also suggest you go through the process more than once because you'll gain more clarity each time.

Remember that the Protector's job is to keep you emotionally and physically well, and your goal is to practice new ways of responding as your Protector stops sabotaging you and becomes your champion.

1.  Decide on one situation or area of your life that is giving you concern or has you in crisis mode.

2.  Think about the most upsetting/disturbing/bothersome/conflictual aspect of the situation and how you feel in it.

3.  Journal about that situation for 5 minutes without censoring your feelings. These are your feelings, and whether or not anyone, including yourself, thinks they are justified they absolutely are. They exist as they are–for now.

4.  Notice what the biggest upset is for you; the part of you that feels the most hurt or angry. Clue: The sentence that keeps repeating in your mind.

5.  Now notice what the voice inside your head is saying. What is that voice trying to protect you from? Hint: feeling hurt, being vulnerable, perceived financial ruin, discomfort, a confrontation.

6.  Now write one to three upsetting things about the situation and one to three ways those events, words, or deeds make you feel (e.g., vulnerable, unjustly blamed, hurt, self-righteous, angry).

7.  Look at those feelings and ask, "What is the hope underneath them?"

8. Then ask yourself, "What's really true?"

This step will reveal what you are trying to avoid knowing or feeling. Read your words. Do you believe the message you are telling yourself? Is it extreme or balanced? Fear is often irrational and shows up in big generalizations that aren't true. So, take a deep breath, get to neutral, and let's get to work.

## PART TWO: Set Your Protector on the Right Course

The Protector is pushing you to respond in a certain way because, at one time in your life it was called into action, rose to the challenge and successfully devised a way to keep you feeling safe. The problem is that you've grown, the situation has changed, and no one told your faithful Protector. Sometimes the Protector is on course. But if it's not, you'll find yourself again and again in situations that appear to keep you safe but are really making you miserable.

## 1. Be Your Own Detective

Let's suppose the situation you picked is one that occurs frequently. Whenever there is a repetitive situation that ends up with the same unsatisfying or negative outcome, history is usually involved in some way. A pattern of thought or behavior has developed. Something in you gets triggered, and you react.

Here comes the detective part:
Look back at what you have written and notice what gets triggered and how you react. Is your gut telling you to be silent, get angry, wait, act, create a façade, look happy, look in control, speak sternly, allow? How do you react? And, finally, what is the hope underneath your feelings and reaction? Quite simply, what are you hoping for?

## 2. Awareness

You've targeted when you get triggered. Now notice your body at that moment. Take a moment to feel it. Where is your body tight, fluttery, dizzy, achy? Notice your body position. These body sensations are your clues–the keys to making something different happen.

## 3. Create Your Vision

Focus on your chosen situation and its message (see Part I, #6). What is your most desired outcome for this situation? Write it down.

IMPORTANT: Write down your perfect outcome, not what you believe is possible.

Now visualize that outcome happening in real-time. You can write it, draw it or see it in your mind's eye.

Often our concerns relate to others in our life. If this is the case, include them in your visualization.

## 4. Now you're ready to practice.

First, imagine the situation. Notice your response and the clues that indicate you're getting triggered. Stop the action and see the vision you want to achieve.

Take a breath. See your vision again.

Hold it in your mind like a precious jewel and define the response you believe will put you on the path to achieving it. See yourself having that response.

Hint: You will have to detach from the habit you've learned over time to allow yourself to have a new response.

## 5. Championing Your Protector

This step is critically important. It's about gratitude and action. After all, your Protector has done you a great service over the years. It has done exactly what it believed was needed, and at some points, it was correct and still is in many situations. But in the situation you have chosen to focus on, it is not. Nevertheless, it has served you steadfastly, honorably, and without hesitation. So now that you've brought what is happening into consciousness and want your Protector to change, it's time for you to take the helm. Having gratitude will help you do it with self-compassion, love, and understanding–and allow you to direct your behavior with confidence, choosing to head in the direction of your vision with your Protector championing, rather than sabotaging you.

I asked you to create an ideal vision. It is working toward that vision that gives us the best real outcome we can hope for because that vision of what you want will become more important to you than winning, hiding, yelling, or stonewalling. That vision will be your guiding light.

The consistent actions you take over time, holding your vision as your guide, is like dropping pebbles into the water of a still pond.

Each time you drop one, it ripples out and changes everything.

Liz Goll Lerner has over 30 years of experience as a coach, counselor, and art therapist. A true pioneer, she's developed many highly respected, groundbreaking psycho-educational and therapeutic programs for her own practice and for health centers across the nation. She was also an adjunct professor at George Washington University and played a pivotal role in a longitudinal study focused on public health for the NIH through Georgetown University's Center on Health and Education.

With certifications in mindfulness practices, energy medicine, and bio-energetics, Liz uses multiple modalities in her integrative practice. Her unique approach is influenced by her deep understanding of the more subtle energies of the body and archetypal psychology. Above all, Liz is committed to creating an integrative, whole-system approach which helps her clients meet their full potential by connecting with their true purpose, putting that purpose into action and healing blocks to growth. She is the creator of Divorce Well and Thrive®; Journey, The Women's Series, and leads many transformational retreats. Her most recent program, Enlightened Communication Through Luminous Living, transforms the way individuals and organizations interact and communicate to help them achieve their goals in even the most high-stakes situations.

For a deeper dive into this chapter go to https://yourinspiredchoices.lpages.co/visioning to enjoy a variety of ways to connect with your vision and your archetypes or reach out to me at https://yourinspiredchoices.com or info@yourinspiredchoices.com

# CHAPTER 18

# Relationship Detox
## Building your Tribe

### BY RONDA LIVINGSTON, PTA-LMT, NCPT

## My Story

If you had asked me 15 years ago what my "tribe" was or who was in it, I likely would have thought you had lost your mind. I did not know then that I'd been purposefully building my tribe for years. Each of us might have a different meaning to the word tribe. When I first started hearing it or paid attention to it, I thought it was some new-age buzz word. But think about it, tribe, village, social circle, family, or whatever you prefer to call it, is the group of people you surround yourself with, in all aspects of your life. These are all meaningful relationships, and they all require investment and thought.

Let's start with family since most of us do precisely that. We begin in our families—whether biological, adopted, or temporary. I'm the youngest of four children born into a poor family. Now, I don't mean just financially poor. I mean love-poor. Financial status is not necessarily indicative of the level of love felt in a home. I've met many people over the years that had financial struggles but always felt loved. I didn't come from one of those homes. Mine was a broken home that no amount of money could've healed.

In my childhood home, our love banks were always overdrawn. My parents held and kept very unhealthy relationships with their family and friends, often making devastating decisions to please my mother's parents. Each of the four of us was born in a different state and endured multiple moves between our births and when we eventually chose to leave and strike out on our own. In those times, we had no choice about who our tribe was, how they interacted with us, or the results of those interactions. We were at the mercy of unmerciful parents, whose decisions were driven by fear, control, substance abuse, and mental illness.

From an early age, this simply didn't *feel* right to me. I couldn't put it into words as a child, but I knew the abuse and neglect we suffered was just not right or how things were supposed to be. By the time my sister was around nine, she was our primary caregiver. She was responsible for getting us up, dressed, and off for school in time to not miss the school bus, so we didn't have to be driven to school. Once we returned from school, it was our responsibility to take care of our household. I don't just mean we had chores. Even the youngest of children can begin to learn responsibility and that things don't magically get done while you sleep. I mean, four young children were handed full responsibilities of running a household—cooking, cleaning, pet care, and taking care of ourselves. That included lawn maintenance and anything else parents usually attend to daily.

My sister was just five years older than I was with two more siblings between us. She was cooking oatmeal for breakfast, standing on an overturned bucket. She did that more times than I could ever remember our mother getting out of bed to care for us. This situation was simply how it was. It bred anger and resentment, often feelings of being abandoned and so many more feelings that I couldn't have defined as a small child. We needed guidance, love, understanding, safety, and many more basics of life that were nearly completely void.

I have few memories of my father in the earlier years. All of my childhood memories until around age nine or ten are scattered and spotty at best, but the ones I have of him usually involve him being drunk and wanting to play and roughhouse while my mother ignored what was happening until one or more of us were hurt. I learned later that he was suffering from PTSD. There was trauma from his years in the military, and he turned to alcohol to soothe his pain. My most frequent memory of my mother was her many ways of escaping the duties of motherhood—sending us outside or sending us to do chores while watching TV or reading romance novels. Any step out of line with her would usually result in her throwing something at us. If we were in reach, one of her favorite methods of gaining uncompromising compliance was by making us stick our tongue out so she could pinch it tightly between her long fingernails where no one could see that we'd been punished. If the infraction were light enough to wait, she would collect them and put my obedient father to the task of doling out our punishment once he returned. They would line us up and yell at us about all the ways we'd broken the rules. We'd then be required to "drop your drawers and grab your ankles" so he could remove his belt and use it against our bare backsides. If we let go of our ankles or "made a scene," we would earn extra licks of the belt.

My youth was my first teacher in terms of feeling the need to distance myself from others. Being raised in that type of environment never helped me learn how to stand up for myself. I never learned that it was not just okay, but important to set boundaries and expect others to treat you well. I sought love from early on and met my husband as a teenager. We were married at 18 and 19 and had our first child when I was just 19. I had no idea what I was doing, but the one thing both of us knew and agreed upon immediately was we could not become like my parents. Thankfully, his parents were concerned for the future of their only grandchild and offered to help. We moved in with them, and through my husband and his family, I began to heal. It was ugly. I was a very angry young woman with very little skills in handling stress. I felt even less love for myself. But oh, the love I had for my child! She softened my anger; she was a true and deep source of love for me. She was my first peek into self-love, and the first thing that sparked that little light in me to listen to that small voice that whispered, *you can be better, you can be loved, you can love.* Her brother's arrival three years later fanned that flame, and, once again, I was astonished at the amount of love a human could feel. They gave me so much courage.

Over the years, my marriage deteriorated into something very unhealthy. The more I grew and became myself, the more I learned and wanted to improve myself, the further apart my husband and I became. We were so young when we began our relationship, and neither of us had the skills or examples of healthy relationships to draw from and emulate. Over time, small disagreements would become big fights. Big fights would become slamming and fits of his rage or things being broken. It never became physically abusive, but I did not feel emotionally safe, loved, or supported in that home. I was always walking on eggshells. I was always afraid to speak my mind because we felt so differently on almost every subject. Differences of opinion could quickly destroy the peace and have myself and our children avoiding interactions with my husband or scattering to anywhere else. I tried to ask for marriage counseling, but my husband didn't think therapy was effective. "That's for crazy people," he'd say. For twenty years, we tried to make it work; neither of us happy. For a long time, I kept telling myself that this was just how marriage was and that there were good parts and to just be thankful for those.

I had been successful at work, both in a banking career and then in health care. I felt I'd found my true calling and that I had value to add to the world. I, most importantly, had been creating connections. I now see how I was drawn to the people who had the qualities I desired. I felt this twisting in my belly when I was around someone dishonest or mean and felt light and airy when in the presence of someone that genuinely cared for others and made an effort to do things to help other people or animals. I started to listen to those feelings in my belly and surround myself with women that inspired me, men that encouraged my strength, and colleagues that were supportive of my growth. I started taking martial arts and grew in a tribe of supportive women who helped me see my worth. With them and my instructor by my side, after several years of training, I earned my 3rd degree Black Belt in Tae Kwon Do. I developed the confidence to leave a terrible job. And all of that blossomed into the courage to leave a broken marriage, go back to school, and push every single day to be and get better. They are my tribe, and I chose them; I choose them every day. You can too!

## MY TOOL FOR YOU

It can be challenging to subjectively view and evaluate the people and influences in your life. The first rule is you're 100% in charge and have all authority to purposefully choose who you allow to influence your mood, your decisions, your victories, and your failures. The rest requires some thought and listening to how something makes you feel. I suggest making lists. I know it sounds silly, but it helps to put a visual together. Again, these things develop over time, and they need to be revisited frequently. If you want to get fancy, you can make a Veen-diagram, but a couple of handwritten lists will be an amazing place to start. There is immeasurable value in writing important things by hand versus typing them out.

The first list I would suggest you make is a list of traits or qualities that you find honorable, desirable, or positive in people—either yourself or others that you respect. This is your **Powerful List** and should be exhaustive—honesty, kindness, courtesy, generosity, confidence—get detailed here. This one should be kind of fun, like a nice dream of all the qualities or ingredients you would use to make your ideal person. Then I want you to make a **Yucky List** (yes, I said yucky because it's a super word). These are all the traits you dislike in people; again, it can be things that you do or those you know. Think of behaviors that make you feel bad or small— dishonesty, judgmental, selfish, narcissism—get equally creative on this list. Write both lists and come back to them a few times, editing, and adding as needed. Be honest. Be brutal. Be open.

This is where it gets a little uncomfortable. Your final two lists may take some additional time and thought. Sit quietly and breathe. Take some time to settle into yourself. Start to create lists of the people in your life that have qualities on either list of attributes. This step can be challenging; take your time. Often, people in your life can be on both lists, and that is okay. Pay attention to your body and how it feels while you go through these steps; it will help guide these exercises. Your intuition will give you little messages, perhaps a feeling in your stomach or your breathing will change signaling stress or anxiety. I encourage you to allow these sensations and witness them without judgment.

For the most challenging aspect of this exercise, start making decisions. Who do you want to be part of your tribe? I attempted early in my adult life to include my parents and to maintain a relationship with them. I finally had to accept that they are who they are. And they don't possess the skills, traits, and characteristics I wish to have in my life and the lives of my children. These can be extremely challenging decisions to make, but you have every right to choose who can play a role in your life. Perhaps it is family, or friends, or work relationships: you can choose your tribe. Also, consider that if you allow someone to take part in your life, you can choose their level of involvement. Think of concentric circles around you; you can place the people in your life as far or as near as you feel comfortable.

Choosing to distance yourself from an unhealthy or toxic relationship is very personal and very individual. I encourage you to take your time, journal about your experiences with the person or persons involved, and truly seek what would give you peace. If better boundaries or creating a little distance between you and the other person can allow the relationship to thrive, then start there first. I didn't take the decision to eliminate a relationship with my parents and the majority of my family lightly. I sought the help of a therapist and leaned on my husband for support. But I know, years later, it was the beginning of becoming me. I know, without hesitation, it was the right decision to make and that it has helped me grow and heal more than any other decision before or since. It gave me strength I didn't know I could possess. That decision helped me build the confidence over the years to leave my broken marriage and a job that was negatively impacting my life.

These are delicate situations and require diplomacy. I'm in no way suggesting that if you are stressed in your work environment, you simply walk out. Make a plan, find a new job, and proceed with grace and professionalism. Look at personal relationships in the same manner. Aside from a dangerous situation, you can often find ways to separate and create space from someone in a gentle way without confrontation. Sometimes this means you must forgo the idea of "closure" or getting an apology and simply move on. Remember, this is about building YOUR tribe, the tribe that'll celebrate your victories, soothe your failures, call you out when you're not doing your best, and everything in between. For additional resources, feel free to visit my website at http://rondalivingston.com/, where I've left some printouts, video links I find helpful, some resources to help you, and stories that dive deeper into my healing journey.

We are the gatekeepers of our own lives. We alone hold the keys to who may access us. This access can look different for each person, from zero contact (as with my parents) to close and loving relationships of all kinds. We're not meant to be unhappy. We're not meant to interact with others when it harms us. Listen to your intuition, make your lists, and feel deeply into what that little voice or guide inside you says. We are the company that we keep. What does your company say about you and who you are as a human and as a person? How does your company have your back? Who are the people you can count on for support and honesty? Who are the people you respect, trust, and look up to? No one tool, trick, or exercise will be able to improve everything. I encourage you to continue to find multiple healthy ways to heal. Put more of the people that align with your **Powerful List** in your inner circle of your tribe and rise with them.

Ronda Livingston is a Physical Therapist Assistant—Expert level Myofascial Release Therapist, Massage Therapist, Nationally Certified Pilates Teacher, Coach, Survivor, and a Healer. Her childhood traumas and experiences launched her into years of personal growth and exploration, seeking to not just heal from her wounds but to help others to heal as well. As a Myofascial Release Therapist, Ronda has witnessed in both herself and her patients the effects of traumas, old and new, both physical and emotional, as well as their very close interconnectedness. Emotional trauma often creates physical manifestations and vice versa, and repeated traumas can have lasting impacts for a lifetime if not addressed.

Ronda believes that healing is multi-level and requires a multi-directional approach and applies that theory in her daily patient care practice as well as her self-care. She combines movement theories, manual therapy, as well as coaching to help people find their balance—literally and figuratively. Her martial arts background taught her to find her voice and use it to help others grow and find theirs. A firm believer that life is meant to be LIVED, not just dreamed about, Ronda continually seeks ways to deepen her knowledge of herself and what she can do to extend a hand to others that may have walked similar paths.

Ronda is not only a survivor of childhood abuse and trauma but a "thriver" as an adult. Her drive to get the most out of life, let go of her past, offer a better life experience to her children, and embrace all the beauty that life has to offer has guided her through big challenges. These include fighting to complete high school (graduating as valedictorian with her newborn in her arms), returning to school not once, but twice, changing careers, and furthering her education in healing. The practice outlined in this chapter has been one of the foundations of building a beautiful and fulfilling life filled with amazing relationships.

When not teaching, healing, or writing, Ronda can be found outdoors exploring nature, fishing, kayaking, paddle-boarding, cycling, or traveling to hike, and sometimes dancing at a kick-ass music festival. She deeply values both her connections to and time spent with other loving people as well as her solo time taking in the silence. You can connect with Ronda at http://rondalivingston.com/, https://www.instagram.com/ronda.liv.heals/ and https://fb.me/Ronda.liv.heals

# CHAPTER 19

# Aromatherapy
## Release Limiting Beliefs with Essential Oils

### BY ANDREA R WARREN AIA, CHWC, CH, ART

Limiting beliefs are stories we tell ourselves, stories that affect every aspect of our lives, from personal to professional. If you're not sure what they are, here are a few of my favorites:

- ◆ I am not smart enough.
- ◆ I am not pretty enough.
- ◆ I do not deserve love.
- ◆ I cannot imagine myself as being successful.
- ◆ I do not want people to think I am...

## My Story

### WHERE THEY START

These beliefs can come from family members, friends, coaches, teachers, and even culture. My introduction to limiting beliefs started early, as far back as kindergarten. I had a lot going on during my first year of primary school. Around this time, I also became acquainted with my first therapist (there were many; I had a knack for wearing them out); he told my parents I was extremely bright, but my hyperactivity was going to limit me. Today they would have diagnosed me with ADHD with a sprinkle of "My fucking parents are getting divorced," with just a dash of "My family is imploding." Negative belief one, check! In these early years, those beliefs were created by others. Oh, but when I was ready, I grabbed that pen and kept writing.

When I eventually picked up the pen, these stories were part of me, they defined me, and I was completely attached to them. Each time an opportunity would arise, my limiting beliefs showed up too. Usually, they would serve up something simple things like, *wait, Andrea, remember you are not polished enough*, or if they really wanted to fuck things up, they would come at me a little more aggressively like, *hey dumbass, what in the Hell are you thinking? You are NOT smart enough!* The latter usually worked; I carried these thoughts around with me for decades.

## LET THE REWRITE BEGIN

About seven years into my marriage, I began to understand that these stories were not serving me; they were not even true. I had to start the process, but where should I begin? The beginning? UGH! I was so over rehashing that shit, and I needed a new technique. Traditional therapy wasn't the answer. About this time, I was introduced to "inner work." Inner work is a spiritual practice of going deep into the self. The purpose of this deep dive is self-exploration, transformation, and, most importantly, healing. I was not going to go it alone, but most of the work was on me, and I was totally okay with that concept.

As I began to dive into those cold dark waters of exploration, I quickly realized I was not prepared. There is one thing I want to convey here; please make sure you are ready because if you are not, the rewrite will turn into one heck of a shit show, and you can add another ten chapters of limiting beliefs. That is precisely what happened to me! Once I faced my ill-preparedness, I began my journey again. This time I came prepared; I was armed with my journal, a few meditations, and a couple of essential oils. I knew I had to go deep into my subconscious mind and was confident the only way to get there was meditation coupled with a powerful blend of essential oils.

Wait. What? Essential oils? When did they come in? At about this time, I had been working with essential oils for close to eight years but had yet to experience their powers in the realm of spiritual healing. I had only used them to create healthy skincare products, and they were the occasional assistant for a sore ankle. When I read my first book about how essential oils can tap into the limbic part of the brain, jostle stored memories, and give us the ability to release trauma, you best believe I was all in.

I used my oils daily, meditated most days, and wrote in my journal a lot. Half the time I had no idea why certain elements showed up, I just kept inflow, dumped what I needed, and moved on. I continued this process for several years and still do. If I told you I was done, I would be lying. My rewrite continues even today as I share this with all of you. You might think, *damn, that is a long-ass time to be releasing limiting beliefs, should I even try this technique?* Even the most highly spiritual people have moments when they feel "off," which is why meditation is part of their daily practice.

We all need an outlet to release the "shit;" it's not only limiting beliefs, but it could also be something as simple as a bad day or a heated argument with a partner. If I'm honest, tools for release of any kind are imperative for our growth and sanity. We need a way to let it all go, whatever "it" is for us. I also want to remind you to not go at it alone. I am blessed to have a group of friends who have stood alongside me and held my hand when I need it. Knowing I was not alone made the dark times easier.

My releasing may continue, limiting beliefs may show up at the least opportune moments, but the good news is I'm now armed with the tools to create a full rewrite when I need it!

## ALL ABOUT CHOOSING WHAT WORKS FOR YOU

Finally, when we talk about "how to" release trauma, there are so many different techniques, and choosing the right one can be overwhelming. Here are a few aspects to consider when you are trying to discern which protocol is proper for you.

◆ Make sure you are ready to start this process. There is a repeat option if you need it.

◆ Find a trained professional to guide through the process.

◆ Work out a plan that speaks to what you are comfortable doing.

◆ Do not rush it! Give yourself all the time you need.

◆ Change direction when needed. You may find that once you choose a technique, it may not serve you throughout the process, so change it.

◆ Tell the people in your life that you are working through some "stuff" (details are not important) and could use their support.

◆ Lastly, be gentle with yourself. This is a process, and it takes time.

Unpacking and releasing our limited beliefs will enable you to live a more meaningful life full of confidence and purpose. It is time for you to start your rewrite!

## The Tool

### THE ART OF THE RELEASE

The Alternative Release Technique (ART) identifies blocks and limiting beliefs through a step-by-step process and provides tools that are needed to release them. Once released, ART then guides toward the creation of an entirely new set of beliefs. As these beliefs unfold, each one can be paired with Young Living essential oils to solidify and create emotional attachment.

## YOU WILL NEED A FEW THINGS BEFORE WE GET STARTED:

- Notebook and Pen
- Cedarwood Essential Oil (this will help you tap into the subconscious mind)
- Vetiver Essential Oil (will help provide clarity)
- Bergamot Essential Oil (provides a release from these beliefs)
- Black Spruce (provides an anchor and gives roots to your new beliefs)

You may also use Ylang Ylang for the anchor step.

I also would recommend that during this practice, you diffuse a blend of calming oils like lavender, sandalwood & myrrh.

Let's get started. First, check your surroundings, make sure you are in a place where you feel comfortable, the temperature is good, lighting is correct, and so on. Now, get into a seated position. I prefer to be in a chair with my feet firmly planted. Once you're seated, close your eyes and take three to four deep cleansing breaths. Do your best to quiet your mind, focusing on this moment in time and letting go of what might be weighing you down.

## STEP 1

Grab the bottle of Cedarwood essential oil. Add two drops in the palm of your hand. Rub your hands together, cup them over your nose, and take a big deep breath in. Repeat this three times.

Cedarwood taps into the conscious and subconscious mind. This will allow your mind to reveal the limiting belief that at this moment is holding you back. If you're struggling, here are a few questions you may want to ask yourself:

- What does this block/limited belief look like?
- When it shows up, how does it feel?
- Where is it limiting me in my life? (relationships, business, and goals)

♦ Is it manifesting itself in other ways? (illness, depression, anxiety)

♦ Be as specific as you can. Once you have identified it, focus on what it will look like once it's released. Imagine it and think of where you will be, who you'll be with etc. Write it down. Be descriptive; use colors, smells, landscapes, etc.

♦ It's important once you've recognized the belief stop there and sit with it. Do not try to release more than one at a time. This is a process, and trying to do too much too fast will not allow for a full release.

♦ Remember you can repeat this as many times as you need.

## STEP 2

Now that you've identified this limiting belief, it's time to get some clarity around the why. Grab the Vetiver essential oil, place two drops in the palm of your hand, rub your hands together, and take a big deep breath in. Do this three times or more if needed. As you breathe in, go back to a time where you first felt this limiting belief or block.

Ask yourself the following questions:

1. How does it make me feel?
2. Where do I feel it in my body?
3. How do I see it showing up in my life now?
4. What is my inner voice saying to me about this belief?

As you answer each of these questions, be aware of how you feel, where you feel it and envision yourself releasing it. Take all the time you need here; again, do not rush it.

At this point in the process, difficult memories are sometimes unearthed, so be gentle and feel the emotions coming up. Continue to breathe slowly. Once you think that you have pinpointed the genesis of this limiting belief, write it down and prepare for the next step.

## STEP 3

Let the release begin! Take your bottle of Bergamot essential oil and add a few drops to the palm of your hand. Breathe in allowing the oil to wash over you, with your eyes closed to focus on the limiting belief. Here is an example:

+ I AM NOT ENOUGH.
+ Say the words I AM NOT ENOUGH
+ Remember the times when you felt it.

Add another drop of Bergamot to the palms of your hands, place them over your nose, and breathe in again. As you breathe out, say:

+ I release (name or phrase of the limiting belief).

Continue this for as many times as you need to. There is no exact number, stay focused on only this belief and breathe it out of existence. As you breathe it out of existence, go back to the image you created in step one of what it will look like once released. Feel that release, call into existence new powerful beliefs.

## STEP 4

Creating a new belief and rooting it. You have released an old belief and blockage, so it is time to create a new one. Before you begin with the essential oils, I want you to state this new belief out loud.
A few examples:

I AM WORTHY
I AM CONFIDENT
I AM POWERFUL
I AM ENOUGH

Once you have your, "I AM" statement clear, write it down.
Please stand-up, take your shoes and socks off. (I prefer to be outside) and firmly plant your feet.
Take out your Black Spruce essential oil, pour two drops in

the palm of your hand, breathe in deeply and repeat your "I AM" statement.

Shout it. Feel it into your body. Harness it. Make it part of you, and root it.

Write this "I AM" statement down and place it on your laptop, bathroom mirror, or tape to a place where you can see it daily.

Now, for those times where those damn old beliefs rear their ugly heads, here is a quick "get the Hell out of here" mindset shift you can do.

Take out your favorite essential oil (this will be your limiting beliefs kryptonite).

Find a quiet place, grab your superpower essential oil, add a few drops in the palm of your hands, rub them together, breathe in and repeat:

I AM IN ALIGNMENT
I AM POWERFUL
I AM ROOTED
I AM WORTHY OF ALL THINGS

And finally, I AM A MAGNET FOR THE EXPERIENCES I MOST DESERVE.

Essential Oils are Nature's Way of Speaking to Our Soul.
    –Andrea R Warren

---

Andrea R Warren is a holistic health and essential oils expert who made her life about learning the facts, gaining the experience, and practicing the secrets you need to feel good, for over 15 years. As an alternative health researcher, holistic practitioner, and skilled aromatherapist she empowers people to take charge of their health and emotional well-being. She'll teach you how to tune into your own experiences and intuition to find what works in order to restore peak balance and optimal wellness. www.AndreaRWarren.com

# CHAPTER 20

# The Art of Self-Care
## Curating Essential Daily Rituals

### BY KRISTI H. SULLIVAN

What do your self-care rituals look like? Do you even have one? And I don't mean drinking a glass of wine each night to unwind—or scrolling through Facebook to take your mind off stress.

The self-care I'm talking about is the real kind—that serves you in a healthy way. Like consuming nourishing foods to give you energy, and drinking enough water. Like spending time with people who inspire you and enrich your life. Like being kind to yourself and setting boundaries. And real self-care is not just exercise and diet. It's so much more—it's self-love.

## My Story

The information I am sharing with you comes from the evolution of my self-love through my self-care efforts. And believe me when I tell you, the journey wasn't always easy for me—and sometimes it's still hard. But self-care did help me get through life-changing challenges and still helps me evolve every day to a deeper level of self-love.

In the last few years, I faced three major crises in my family, marriage, and career. I felt panic and fear about things I couldn't control, struggled with depleted energy, and was concerned about the short and long-term effects on my physical and mental well-being. I'm sure you can identify with this. I now know that my self-care tools and habits helped me get through these life-changing challenges.

I believe that self-care is essential for women more than ever to evolve mind-body-spirit, and I'm proud to commit to self-care daily. And I know the importance of support to make this happen. So I'm on a mission to help busy women give themselves permission to make self-care a priority. I guide, motivate, and educate women to curate daily self-care rituals that fit their lifestyle through a community of like-minded women and a network of healing resources and tools.

Let me share with you how this mission evolved.

It was a year that brought me to my knees. I'm sure you may know the kind of year that I'm describing—when one thing after another just seems to happen, challenge after challenge, without life letting up—the type of year that you're thankful to have over when the New Year's Eve ball drops. Not once but twice that ball drop didn't turn the page to a fresh start for me, it only seemed to bring another challenge.

Between 2018 and 2020, I faced a family crisis, a marriage crisis, and a job crisis—each an unexpected situation, and each creating intense emotions and trauma. In that somewhat short period, I experienced sadness, grief, despair, frustration, anger, rage, panic, and even PTSD (my definition of it). I felt broken and shattered into pieces, and at times, beyond any hope of repair or recovery.

In 2018, I got a startling phone call in the middle of the night, waking me from my sleep. It was my mother in a panic that I had never heard before. My father, who had Alzheimer's for many years (a late-age diagnosis with a slow progression), awakened my mother and dragged her out of bed while frantically yelling, "We need to leave, we need to leave!" in his native Polish tongue. The situation was so terrible that the police and EMTs had to intervene, resulting in a visit to the hospital. The phone call I received that night triggered fear, lack of control, and anxiety that I never experienced before.

Later that year, my nearly 20-year marriage began to unravel. For several months, we lived apart, and I told barely anyone as I lost my sense of trust and faced uncertainty about the future of a marriage I had defined. I can only describe it now as avalanches of hurt, shame, and despair that rocked my world over and over for more than a year, while our foundation crumbled with heart-wrenching loss.

Fast forward to the beginning of 2020, I sat down with a new boss for my annual job review. I was about to celebrate my 20th anniversary at a job I held on to, and an identity I was attached to for far too long—only to find out shockingly that I was getting eliminated from the company, which had been like family to me. Not only did I feel the floor suddenly go out from under me, but I felt anger, disappointment, and grief that this was happening and because I didn't get to leave on my terms.

And then COVID happened. While some feel COVID forced us to be in isolation, disrupted our routines, and created overwhelm, I realized the opportunity to slow down, practice being in solitude, and turn inward to learn the effects of this global situation. I began to understand what I needed to get through this unfamiliar crisis. This happened during a time I also realized the essential need for my daily self-care.

I've learned that my saving grace through challenging times is my self-care—finding a way as often as I can to pay attention to my body, mind, and spirit. The self-care practice I had established before I faced my crises helped me get through those life-altering events. I, fortunately, had a 20-year-long history of practicing yoga, which only was the beginning. Thankfully, yoga taught me about the mind-body-spirit connection, and eventually, I explored and practiced various modalities to heal the wounds, self-limiting beliefs, and past traumas.

## The Tool

I believe there are three levels of self-care to help you heal, reprogram, and evolve your mind, body, and spirit. These three levels of self-care are:

1. Occasional self-care—periodic, time-bound, or sporadic activity
2. Daily self-care—commitment to everyday activities
3. Spiritual self-care—deeper, long-lasting actions to evolve and heal

Level 1—Occasional self-care means you may sporadically exercise, sometimes have periods of eating well, and once in a while take time to slow down (like a vacation). The payoff is short, and effects are rarely long-lasting. Most individuals may start a self-care routine with the occasional practice. This category includes New Year's resolutions that are usually cast by the wayside after a few weeks.

Level 2—Daily self-care means you are committed to following a more regular, consistent schedule—like moving your body in some way for 30 minutes a day, or choosing vegetables and fruits as your daily main food groups. And perhaps going to bed at a reasonable time to get enough sleep, to rejuvenate and feel rested every morning. While individuals at this level may sometimes have the occasional slip (a late night, or sweet treat, or a day skipping exercise), they go right back to a daily routine because they are (key word) "committed" and have created recurring habits.

Level 2 sounds ideal and is sometimes the level we aim for achieving—where we set our goal and consider it accomplished if we are committed. BUT I'm challenging you today to set the bar higher because the pay off is much bigger, longer-lasting, and life-changing!

Level 3—Spiritual practice means you are connected to a higher power or your inner wisdom, or ultimately aligned in mind-body-spirit and self-love. In addition to your daily mind-body activity, you also explore what's on the inside. Perhaps it's through journaling, keeping a daily gratitude diary, or praying. Or it's working with a practitioner to address limiting beliefs or old wounds from trauma (which we all have, by the way). It's slowing down and turning attention from the outside inward to explore how you can evolve even deeper and more fully to expand not only self-love but to become a light to others. Level 3 is BIG.

It may seem like a lofty aspiration, a dream to become enlightened. But friends, we are all spiritual beings having a human experience—and what does life mean if not a journey for us to evolve fully mind, body, and spirit? I urge you to consider which level you are at. You might ask yourself, *is it really serving you to your fullest potential?*

Are you at level 1, occasional or sporadic? Or level 2, committed daily? Or can you reach for level 3—a deeper, spiritual practice?

Self-care can help you heal, reprogram, and evolve. Real self-care will expand your mind, body, and spirit. Self-love can change you—and the world. As Gandhi said, be the change. We need you and each other more than ever to be the light to lead the way.

I know for me, I survived some pretty serious times of crisis because I used self-care tools and resources that I learned before I faced these challenges. It's why my mission is to motivate and educate others to make self-care a daily ritual. Now is your time for self-love!

## YOUR VISUAL SELF-CARE PLAN:

### *How to Create a Mind Map to Curate Daily Self-Care Rituals*

Step 1: Prepare items to create a visual self-care plan—gather paper and pens/pencils (colored to make it even more creative). You may also want to have magazines, scissors, and glue (or tape) to make your mind map more like a vision board once you've created the main components of the plan.

Step 2: Find some quiet time to sit in a place that is relaxing or serene. Take a few deep breaths to get centered. Let go of any distractions from the day, or to-dos that are on your mind. Perhaps listen to a short meditation to help you become present and focused in your body (and out of your head).

Step 3: Use one sheet of paper to journal in a free-flow manner the following—on one side, write down the reasons you want to create self-care in your life (e.g., *why is it important to you now, what are you looking to achieve with the self-care, what are you hoping to create through more self-care, how do you want to improve your life using self-care*). On the other side of the paper, write down the challenges you have (e.g., *what are any blocks to your self-care, what are the reasons you haven't done more self-care, what is keeping you stuck from doing self-care, how have limiting beliefs or actions affected your self-care*). The purpose of this journaling is to help empty your mind of thoughts—both conscious and unconscious.

Step 4: Take a few breaths (from the diaphragm or deep belly) to let go of the journaling exercise and become more present and connected to your inner wisdom. Call in your higher power (universe, God—use the words or concepts that speak to you), guides and angels, even loved ones that have passed, to help the process of allowing your inner wisdom to create the plan that best serves you at this time.

Step 5: Ask yourself what word represents self-care to you—this can be an emotion, a theme, an idea, or else simply use the phrase "self-love." On a blank sheet of paper, write that word in the center of the paper in large/bold font. This will be the center of your mind map; let's call it your intention.

Step 6: Draw lines that branch off of the center word and write words that represent different aspects of your center word—these could include steps or actions that support your intention (e.g., exercise, being in nature, journaling, dancing, meditation, tapping, massage). If desired, draw secondary lines that branch off to support your steps/actions further. Also, if desired, be creative and add visual photos/pictures, stickers, or simply color to the overall mind map.

Step 7: On a new piece of paper, create of list of action items that you would like to do on a daily, weekly, and monthly basis. You may also identify steps that need to be done in the short term (2-4 weeks) as well as longer-term (1-3 months) to support your regular self-care practices.

Congratulations—this mind map is now your customized plan to curate daily self-care rituals!

**Resources: Visit www.kristisselfcare.com for more information about this mind map process and additional resources to support your self-care.**

---

Kristiana H. Sullivan is a self-care expert with a passion for health, wealth, and happiness—and helping women thrive in these areas. She began her journey nearly two decades ago as a yoga teacher (RYT200) and entrepreneur while culling her communication skills at nonprofit environments in Connecticut. During COVID, Kristi took her business online and now hosts a virtual membership community to connect busy women to resources and support for curating daily self-care rituals. In addition to hosting wellness workshops and webinars, she also teaches audiences about Human Design and the art of aligning with your true self for manifesting abundance. Kristi encourages her clients and students to be inspired and empowered, and also enjoys sharing her marketing background to guide like-minded, holistic practitioners to change the world.

# CHAPTER 21

# Wilderness Medicine
## Abdominal Pain: Serious or Not?

### BY SUSAN PURVIS, WEMT

## My Story

A day at the ski clinic treating more than thirty patients with an assortment of ailments including double wrist fractures, a boot-top crack, an outbreak of herpes simplex viral infection on the lips, and a couple of "I don't feel so goods," wears me out.

With minimal time to pee or eat, my patience wanes to the verge of fraying. Two-year-old Tasha, my certified avalanche dog, lies on the waiting room carpet with her head between her front paws. "I know. It's been a long day."

Hours beyond her normal feeding time, she had already hounded me by nibbling her front teeth up and down on my lower pant leg, as if she is fleecing me or eating corn on the cob. She senses the difficulty of the day.

I look up to our last patient. The young woman coughs up frothy pink sputum into a plastic bucket. By my second season at the clinic that sits at 9500 feet above sea level, I've seen the same symptoms plenty of times.

Tasha's tail thumps the floor once, as she watches me turn back to work on the woman. On this day, Dr. Tom is away in Aspen performing surgery. Dr. Tom, the owner of the clinic, trusts me enough to keep an eye on the new guy, the practitioner in charge—Scott Smith, a physician's assistant, recently arrived from Maine and with years of ski trauma and rescue experience.

Standing at the door of the coughing woman's room, Scott plans to give her Tylenol for what he diagnoses as a cold or bronchitis. He intends to send her home to her ski condo at 10,000 feet for the night. I foresee tragedy.

"Scott, wait." I grab his arm before he enters the room. My voice crackles as I summon the bravery to tell him something he might not want to hear. After all, I'm an Emergency Medical Technician, not a physician.

"Yeah?" He squares his shoulders.

"Um...ah, I know we've had a big day, and it's late. But ..." I pull him toward me, so the patient can't hear my words. To reassure myself, I eye the patient's chest x-ray hanging in the lightbox. Healthy lung tissue on x-ray normally looks black. This woman's tissue is snow-white, and the lungs are full of fluid. She lives at sea level, but she's skiing at 11,000 feet. If I don't say something, she will drown in her own fluid tonight at her condo.

The sudden raspy cough, pink, frothy sputum, fever, weakness, and rapid heart rate confirm my diagnosis: High Altitude Pulmonary Edema (HAPE), an illness we frequently see at the clinic. HAPE happens at high altitudes. The only cure is transporting the patient to a lower elevation. The oxygen I have been giving her isn't helping. The woman must go to the hospital in Gunnison, seventeen hundred feet below the clinic.

I face Scott. The uber-smart, driven perfectionist now carries a streak of Napoleon complex on his tense, short frame. My experience in the clinic doesn't measure up to his fifteen years as a physician's assistant, his decade of ski trauma work, and his position as curriculum director at the largest wilderness medical organization in the world. He has preached to thousands of students the dangers of HAPE, yet on this day, he fails to recognize a classic example in the coughing woman.

From behind the wall, the young woman sits up to cough. Her inhalation rattles from fluid stuck in her chest. She gasps, coughs again, and falls back into the gurney.

"Scott. That lady can't stay here. We need to call her an ambulance and get her to Gunnison. She's got HAPE." There, I said it. I mustered the courage to intervene. I hold my breath for his response.

In the silence, Scott scratches his head. Glancing at the x-ray, he spins from me toward the reception room. His footsteps circle the clinic floor. Tasha's eyes follow, and I prepare for a thrashing. I just questioned his authority, his position, his knowledge. I'm dead. Or at least soon to be unemployed.

He faces me. "You're right, Sue. I've been teaching this stuff for years, and I couldn't see it in front of me. Respiratory distress! How could I have missed that?!"

The air leaves my body in one big exhale, and my shoulders lower as tension dissipates. A weak smile twitches my mouth.

Scott adds, "You just saved her life."

## FINDING PURPOSE AND PASSION

The year was 1997 when I first found the courage to speak up and save that woman's life. That was 23 years ago. I was 34, searching for passion and purpose, and questioning my career as a gold exploration geologist in the Dominican Republic with my husband.

Scott became influential in my search for purpose when our friendship and respect grew on that cold and snowy night while we treated the woman for respiratory distress. He saw something in me that I couldn't see in myself. Over the next decade, while I worked at the clinic and became his wilderness medicine teaching assistant, Scott mentored me. "You don't have to go to medical school to understand medicine," he told me. I quickly realized knowledge is power, and I could help and heal patients using my Emergency Medical Technician skills.

He taught me the general principals of pathology, physiology, structure, and function of the human body. His simple explanations of how the major body systems work empowered me to learn as much as I could about medicine. The application of these principals applies to both urban and wilderness settings.

Scott had a lot to teach me. Little did I know my life would move toward medicine.

I traded my rock hammer as a geologist looking for gold in Latin America for a pair of skis and a chance to save a life. I chased a career as a wilderness and rescue medicine specialist working in the ski clinic, as a professional ski patroller, an ambulance medic, a search and rescue team K-9 handler, a ski guide, and a wilderness medicine educator. I opened Crested Butte Outdoors, my outdoor education company, which specializes in wilderness medicine and avalanche education. My dog Tasha and I became one of the top high-altitude search dogs in Colorado. We found people buried in avalanches, submerged in the water, and lost in the mountains. After Tasha died, I wrote *Go Find: My Journey to Find the Lost—and Myself* about our career together in Colorado and how, in the end, she saved my life.

## PAYING IT FORWARD

One of the most useful things I learned from Scott was the generic structure and function of the abdomen (the stuff inside your stomach). I've been teaching this lecture for twenty years, and this knowledge helped me become a more skillful practitioner. I want you to know this because knowledge is power. If you find yourself in a remote area or even in an urban setting and have abdominal pain, here is a tool to determine if you need to seek immediate medical care.

# The Tool

## THE DIFFERENCE BETWEEN SERIOUS AND NOT SERIOUS ABDOMINAL PAIN

When you die, you either die of shock, respiratory failure, or brain failure. The woman with HAPE could have died that night of respiratory failure, then brain failure, had we sent her back to the ski condo. Soon after the HAPE incident, I learned about shock, the other thing that can kill you. It was an early morning at the clinic when a healthy, athletic man in his 40's stumbled in and groaned, "Help me. I think I'm going to die." Doubled over in pain, he looked pale, sick, and was breathing fast. "This pain won't go away."

"What the heck happened to you?" I asked, escorting the patient to the gurney. "Did you fall?" I had no idea what was wrong with him. I had never seen serious abdominal pain before. Upon examination, Scott bumped the gurney purposefully. Immediately, the patient screamed, "What the fuck?" Then he doubled over to protect his lower guts.

"This guy needs bright lights and cold steel," Scott shouted at me, his signal that the patient needs to see a surgeon now. "Call the ambulance, Sue."

Later, I asked, "How did you know he had serious abdominal pain?"

"Susan, he presented with most red flags for serious abdominal pain." As a wilderness medical practitioner, Scott had to be satisfied with the generic assessment; serious or not serious. I did not matter what the cause.

The word abdomen in Latin means hidden. If you show up into the ER with generic stomach pain, making a specific diagnosis can be a challenge for experienced clinicians, even when using laboratory data and sophisticated imaging equipment. Doctors can't tell if you are suffering from early cholecystitis, diverticulitis, gastroenteritis, menstrual cramps, an extra helping of Thanksgiving dinner, constipation, or a big ole fat fart. The question is, how do we tell the difference between serious and not serious abdominal pain?

## GENERAL PRINCIPAL OF WILDERNESS MEDICINE—OBSTRUCTION TO INFECTION

I learned there are basically three major structures inside the abdomen: hollow organs, solid organs, and the peritoneum.

If you obstruct a hollow organ long enough, it will become

infected. Here is why. The human body is full of hollow organs that store, transport, or excrete fluids of all types. These include sweat glands, intestines, bladder, and all the associated ducts. If the drainage from these organs is obstructed by swelling, deformity, or a foreign body, the accumulation and pressure cause inflammation and pain.

If the obstruction persists, any bacteria present can begin to grow out of control in whatever substance is trapped, and infection will develop. Take, for example, a zit on the face. A sweat gland is an external hollow organ infection becoming obstructed. Appendicitis is a more serious example of the same pattern. If that infection is inside your abdomen, like in the case of appendicitis, there is no place for the infection to go except into your abdominal cavity. Hollow organ infection inside the abdomen can kill you, and you die of shock. Many illnesses have their origins in obstruction, and their cure is in relieving it.

### Hollow organs

Hollow organs in the abdomen have a lot of nerves, and when stretched, it hurts. You may have felt it before after your stomach or intestines distend after eating a giant tub of popcorn. You vow never to do it again, but you do. Stretching a hollow organ stimulates muscular contraction, causing the pain of distention to become worse, but temporarily. We call this generalize crampiness that comes and goes. The pain is non-specific, poorly localized at the general level of nerve innervation. Because peristalsis (the excretion and movement of fluids and food through the digestive system using rhythmic muscle contractions) increases the pain in waves, the discomfort tends to be intermittent. This type of abdominal pain--intermittent, non-specific, and generalized is less likely to be serious. This non-serious abdominal pain is usually associated with conditions that are well contained within the hollow organs, not affecting the abdominal cavity itself.

Besides hollow organs, what else is in the abdominal cavity?

## Peritoneum

If you were to dissect the peritoneum from the body, it would fill the surface area of half a tennis court. This huge, beautiful membrane lines the abdominal wall and surrounds the guts allowing them to move around freely. The peritoneal lining can be irritated by bacteria, blood, and digestive fluids that have leaked into the abdominal cavity. When inflamed, the peritoneum gets pissed-off and tells you about it. "It hurts right there." The patient will complain of severe pain that is localized, constant, and aggravated by movement and palpation. With inflammation, a person can lose a large volume of fluid in a short period of time, and this causes volume shock. Likewise, if the hollow organ contents continue to spill out of the container, it will spread through the abdomen. Shock and death are often the result. Peritoneal signs indicate a serious abdominal problem regardless of the location or cause.

## Solid Organs

The liver, spleen, and kidneys are like blood-filled baby watermelons hanging inside of the abdomen. They have a variety of functions and associated diseases, but we worry most about their potential for rupture in abdominal trauma. Unlike hollow organs, solid organs have few nerve endings that sense pain. Most of the discomfort with solid organ problems come from irritation of the organs peritoneal lining due to infection or bleeding. Both are serious. Solid organs, if hit hard enough, enough to knock the wind out of you, can fracture and bleed on impact. The abdomen offers a large enough space into which blood can be lost to cause volume shock. This event can be fatal. As a first responder, one should be alert to the development of peritoneal signs following significant blunt trauma to the abdomen. With constant pain and localized tenderness, volume shock from internal bleeding is the anticipated problem.

## CONCLUSION

Real problems begin when whatever is happening inside the gut begins to irritate the peritoneal lining inside the abdomen. In the case of our 40-year-old patient, his problem started with obstruction to infection principal of the appendix (hollow organ), in his lower right abdomen. We found in the patient's history that two days prior, he complained of generalized cramps and discomfort typical of hollow organ stretching. He felt sick, stopped eating, and brushed it off to an upset stomach. No need to seek urgent care as a doctor would have said, "Come back in if you have signs of serious abdominal pain." By the next morning, the crampiness changed to local pain as the appendix continued to swell and slowly leak. Luckily for the patient, his hollow organ didn't completely burst and spill digestive enzymes and pus onto his entire abdominal cavity. That event may have killed him. Instead, he sought medical care just in time. He presented at the clinic with persistent, localized pain and signs and symptoms of shock: high heart and respiratory rate, fever, pale, cool, and clammy skin. The appendix was swollen, pressing against the peritoneum, perhaps leaking and ready to burst wide open. His quick action to seek medical help saved his life. So it doesn't matter if you're in the woods, at home, or in the clinic, recognition of serious abdominal pain is the key to recognizing a life-threatening problem. The treatment of a serious intro-abdominal problem requires a hospital and surgical care. Evacuation should be urgent.

## ABDOMINAL PAIN RED FLAGS

Serious:
♦ Persistent fever
♦ Bloody vomit or diarrhea
♦ Constant, localized pain and tenderness
♦ Fast pulse and respiratory rate, pale, cool and clammy skin.
♦ Lasts more than 24 hours

## TREATMENT FOR SERIOUS ABDOMINAL PAIN

## Anticipate

- ♦ Volume shock
- ♦ Systemic infection

## Treatment

- ♦ Keep the patient comfortable
- ♦ Maintain hydration
- ♦ Maintain body core temperature
- ♦ Restrict foods to easily absorbed sugars
- ♦ Emergency evacuation

If you'd like to learn more about shock, respiratory distress, changes in brain function or serious abdominal pain, and its application in the wilderness, check out one of Susan's upcoming wilderness medicine courses and special retreats at www.cboutdoors.com.

Interested in Susan's Wilderness Adventures Newsletter? Susan's Resource page? If so, sign up by logging onto www.susanpurvis. com. The first part of her essay is from an excerpt from her best-selling memoir, Go Find: My Journey to Find the Lost—And Myself, published by Blackstone. Susan also narrates her audiobook.

A big thanks goes out to Wilderness Medical Associates for the use of their teaching materials.

---

Susan Purvis saves lives and teaches others to do the same. She's explored the hottest, highest, and coldest places on the planet as a wilderness medicine specialist, explorer, and educator. Susan's best-selling and award-winning adventure memoir *Go Find: My Journey to Find the Lost—and Myself* tells the story of training and deploying her search dog, Tasha, in the high country of Colorado. She received Congressional Recognition for their role in avalanche search and rescue. In 2019, her book ranked #4 behind Michelle Obama's Becoming. Susan is working on her second book and a Go Find screenplay. She's a member of the prestigious *Explorers Club*, an international multidisciplinary professional society with the goal of promoting scientific exploration and field study, and just one of 830 women in the world.

Susan is the founder and owner of *Crested Butte Outdoors International*, an outdoor educational company. She's taught wilderness medicine to everyone from the Secret Service to Sherpa guides in Nepal.

Purvis' work has appeared in the *New York Times, Wall Street Journal, Smithsonian,* the BBC, and on Discovery. To read about Susan in the news (videos, articles, and radio), log onto Susan's website at www.susanpurvis.com.

When Susan is not teaching, you can find her boating on the cold, clear rivers in northern Montana or in search of the last snow powder stash.

CHAPTER 22

# Freeing Your Voice
## Healing Through Full Expression of Your Truth

BY DIANNA LEEDER, CPCC

## My Story

I have a tattoo on the inside of my left arm.

No, it isn't snakes, dragons or mythical creatures. And it doesn't say, MOM.

My tattoo says, "Look inside," and it's a reminder to always look inside myself for my voice and what it needs to say. I gotta tell you, there have been days when I really needed that reminder.

I'm not sure I truly knew I had a real voice, or that I was missing anything without it until I was in my 40's. Hmm, clearly a late bloomer!

As a kid, I was never taught that I needed my voice to reflect my needs and desires, other than the obvious livelihood ones. And as the youngest of five, I rarely had to speak for myself when there was always someone to do it for me.

As a result, I grew up not knowing myself very well. With people around me calling the shots, I didn't need to call my own and began to depend on others to show me the way. I relied on their opinions, their advice, and sometimes clear direction to make decisions. By default, I did what was expected of me, rather than consider the very best options for me first.

That worked while I was a kid, but as I faced adulthood, it became increasingly uncomfortable. At the time, although I didn't understand it, I had a consistent longing to be heard and therefore be seen; to stand out as someone different from the crowd. But I had no idea how to put any of that into action in an intentional way.

"Intentional" has become an important word for me. And it's important for you too if your voice has been highjacked or if you don't feel good or safe using it. We've all been in situations where we speak up out of sheer frustration or emotion, but there is little intention behind that kind of outburst. Intentional speaking is being clear and confident about what we need that's requiring our voice to get out. What are we missing? What comfort do we need? What do we want more of? What are we called to stand up for?

What we know about ourselves, in all our beautiful and sassy glory, we can intentionally apply to our everyday lives, including situations where we need to speak up, do something we want to do, or be the person that we need and want to be. When we know ourselves and follow our own direction, we're aligned. There is no longer a shadow person shielding us from what we want; we're healing by being true to ourselves.

I began my career advocating and speaking for other women whose voices were drowned out by abusive partners, the inequities of poverty, and by a society that defined what we could or couldn't do based on our gender. I'm very proud of the community changes I was part of, and that women who worked with me left feeling stronger and more empowered. But the irony isn't lost on me that I would choose a career path voicing other women's pain when I was unable to voice my own.

Years ago, I had a co-worker tell me, "You don't like to be told what to do." Wow. I see now what I couldn't see then. She was right. That was my inner self fighting back, wanting to be voiced.

During that time, I was quite content being a good sister, a good daughter, a good friend, a good life partner, and a good mother. There were parts of all those roles that I loved being. But without knowing my needs well enough to clearly express them, I was following a script of sorts that belonged mostly to people around me. And in my head, my role was to ask, *What does he need? What do they need? What do they expect of me? What am I supposed to be doing?* I blindly played that role, and anytime I started to feel an internal push back, I brushed it off as me just being bitchy.

As women, not knowing ourselves well enough to use our voices confidently and with intention is an easy place to get comfortable. There are still stereotypical roles we're expected to play relative to nurturing and emotionally supporting others. Some of which we're truly drawn to, I mean, who doesn't want to be there for their loved ones?

But when that expectation takes over for our own needs, we can get lost there, and our voices become quieter except the voices in our heads that whisper shame and resentment for feeling anything but satisfied with our caregiving roles.

I landed somewhere between my own needs and the expectations of me and stayed there for some time. Without knowing myself enough to use my voice fully, my roles were only peppered with what I needed and were more about what those around me needed. I have no regrets, I would still move mountains for my loved ones, but after I learned about myself and my needs, my why changed.

When we can't be entirely honest with ourselves, the Universe eventually gets honest with us. You know, the offering of circumstances that we really don't want but cannot ignore.

She was yelling at me to figure out what I needed to change up to experience more of what I really wanted in my life.

"Wtf Universe! What's happening?"

"This is an offering, an opening to what's there for you to experience if you take it," she answered.

"Okay, I get it, and I feel something is missing, but what do I do?"

"You walk down the path opening up in front of you, explore the conflict and pain both inside and outside of yourself. Peek out from behind your own shadow. Take a good look at your needs that aren't being met, and what you can do to be your true and best self."

So I did. That circumstance knocked me on my butt and forever changed how I perceive myself and what's available to me as an independent human being, separate but connected. It turned out what I needed was more clarity, more equality, more sharing of my gifts with humanity, and, most of all, more use of the precious gift of my voice to intentionally express what I needed and wanted; everything I needed and wanted.

It's a tough place to be in one's life. You're wounded. You know you need more because you don't like how you feel, and you don't want to feel that way anymore. You know there is no other way out but through the fear of using your voice and being self-reliant. You feel stuck and scared about what's on the other side of your journey to what feels better.

But you're also pissed. You know that this doesn't define you, that there are so many good parts of your life your strong and capable self has built, so how could all this have happened? It doesn't matter how it happened. The gift is in the work that gets done to make yourself feel whole.

Coaching helped me gain a huge awareness of my needs. It opened me up to myself. During one of our first sessions, my coach asked, "What's important to you, just you?"

*Seriously? I have no idea*, was my first thought. That was so hard to answer, since I had never actually made it a priority to think about before, outside of eating really good chocolate. But I quickly learned it was self-reliance at its best as I dug inside to understand myself and my needs, and use my voice to better frame my relationships, directing my life in ways that made my experiences feel aligned and good.

It helped me create such powerful healing shifts in my life that I trained as a Co-Active Life Coach, and followed with a Confidence certification. I will forever be grateful for learning what self-aware-ness and self-reliance could do for me. Of what I needed to grow and thrive as an independent woman, and of who I needed to be to heal and allow my heart to open up fully.

In my practice, I see countless women who are unable to use their own voices confidently. Often it's about fear of hurting or let-ting someone down and the assumption that they need to choose between honoring themselves and fulfilling the needs of others. Good thing we have love to help us out!

We show ourselves and others great love by expressing our needs with clarity, confidence, and kindness when we say yes, when we say no, or not now, or when we say I am strong enough to do this on my own. It's an even stronger love hit when we express ourselves with the respect that says we are all capable of walking our own path, and that we do no favors by trying to fix or rescue each other.

Many women think they can't use their voices because they don't have enough confidence. Indeed, that fear may be much of what holds us back, but our confidence is in part based on being sure that what we're expressing is factual or true. It's about knowing our topic, knowing our stuff, and sharing it when the need arises. What better thing to be aligned with when speaking up than ourselves, our needs, and what's important to us? Confidently speaking, I think we've got this.

When we feel less than whole, or when we're unable to use our voices, it's because we're disconnected from our understanding of ourselves and misaligned from what we need. We feel that misalignment in our bodies, our heads, and in our hearts. Think muscle tension, headaches, stomach aches, bowel issues, resent-ment, anger, sadness, perfection, comparisons, feeling like we are invisible to others, and fear, of course, just to name a few! It's all us saying, "No."

We question our ability to say and do the things we want to. We question our self-worth and our value. We listen way too much to our inner mean girls. Our relationships suffer because we can't always be honest with others about what we need. We get stuck in that mental rut where decision-making becomes super hard. We compromise our mental and physical health by creating behaviors like avoidance, that we think keep us safe but actually move us further away from our true selves.

Everyone has off days, but we humans are not meant to be misaligned with our needs and desires for any length of time. When that's the case, we're in conflict with ourselves, and there is no peace in conflict.

By knowing ourselves, and then aligning our actions, our behaviors, and our voices with our own truth, we can powerfully stand in that truth to get our needs met.

From there, we can begin to heal.

## The Tool

Welcome to your deep core, where everything about you lives; intel from your body and mind, to heart, and even spirit.

It's all the things you know about yourself already. It's where your unique values live, what your intuition tells you, what's important to you. It's what supports you, what's working for you right now, and why. It's what's happening in your life when you feel fulfilled and content.

And it's where your Inner Goddess hangs out. She's the one who tells you what's in your deep core. I call her the Inner Goddess; you can call her anything you like.

She is your back-up to being the woman you are called to be. She knows what's right for you and what makes you feel amazing. She's part of you; she's the inner voice of you. She *is* you.

### STEP 1: WHO YOU ARE RIGHT NOW?

Grab three pieces of paper. On the first one, make a list of everything you know about yourself, your needs, and what makes you feel fulfilled. What makes you feel good.

You already know all kinds of things through practical experience. Be broad here, don't worry if you think it's trivial or small, like that avocados aren't your friend. Nothing is trivial to your self-understanding. You are the expert in everything about you; it's all part of your foundation for using your voice.

Include your values here too. Values are your principles or standards of behavior that, when honored, leave you feeling fulfilled. Go with your gut, and if you get stuck, you'll find a list of values you can work from here https://cravemorelife.com/resources/.

Here are some questions to help you, use all or some as you like. Don't get stalled on the negative; it's just a way to help you get to the positive.

What doesn't work for you? What makes you resentful? What don't you like? What makes you angry? What are you unwilling to bend on? What are you not getting enough of in your life? What makes you cry? What makes you hurt inside?

What *does* work for you? What keeps you going? What frees you up? What do you like? What is fulfilling? What feels good? What feels successful? What are you getting now in your life that feels great? What makes you laugh? What makes your heart warm?

## STEP 2: CONNECT TO YOUR INNER GODDESS

This is, for the most part, an intuitive practice but not solely. We have noticed what we already know about ourselves, and now we listen to our Inner Goddess for more.

Meditation or quiet reflection are both great ways to connect to your Inner Goddess. As time goes on and you become more proficient at connecting with her, you'll find you'll intuitively know what she is telling you anywhere, anytime.

For now there is a downloadable Inner Goddess Meditation at https://cravemorelife.com/resources/ if you need it.

Or, you can do whatever you're most comfortable with to get to a calm and relaxed place where you can have a conversation with your Inner Goddess. Walk or sit in nature. Be alone in your comfort/pleasure spaces. Be wherever you feel the calmest and most relaxed. Allow yourself this time and space just for you.

From that state of relaxation and chill, tell yourself:

"I am grateful for this time to concentrate on just me,"

"I am trusting my own judgment,"

"I am one with my Inner Goddess to learn what I can about things that serve me, serve my heart, serve my soul, serve my body, serve my mind and serve my spirit."

Now let yourself go deeply inside to find your Inner Goddess and your own answers. Picture her residing inside you. Notice where she lives. Knock on her door and let her make you a cup of tea. Have a conversation with her. Ask her specific questions about what you need to be content and fulfilled, or keep it general. Listen closely to what answers and messages come to you. When you are done, thank your Inner Goddess for taking care of you and always being there, guiding you to be your best self.

Once you have connected to your Inner Goddess and you're ready to come out of the meditation, immediately jot down everything you heard and/or understood about yourself on the second piece of paper.

## STEP 3: CREATE YOUR "ME"

It's time to create a visual of what you now know about yourself. Take the third piece of paper and draw a fun picture of you in the middle, putting your name at the top, leaving lots of room to add text. I'm going to call it your "Me."

Now go back to the first two pieces of paper and circle key words or short phrases that jump out at you as being your true essence. Take those key words and phrases and write them around the picture of you.

This is you. This is your wholeness and your goodness. It's your foundation for creating boundaries, for saying yes and no, for doing meaningful work, for sharing your love in satisfying ways, for being of service to others. It's a work in progress, and as such, you can add to it whenever you like.

It's how you create the feelings of contentment you need to thrive.

Post it on your fridge or bathroom mirror. Take a picture of it and make it your screen saver. Keep it close, so it stays part of your awareness. It's there to inform your thoughts, actions, and behaviors to support your voice going forward.

## STEP 4: STRENGTHENING YOUR VOICE AND EXPRESSING YOUR TRUTH

Now you have your foundation; it's time to use it.

Start from where you are. Your understanding of yourself will have opened your eyes to things that you want to do, want to be, and definitely things you want to say.

Use your "Me" to make a plan for what some of those things might be. Make an agreement with yourself or a friend to express a need each week and work your way up to each day. Every chance you get, voice something you know you need.

Using your voice isn't just about what you say to other people; it's also about what you say to yourself. Use your value of integrity to give yourself what you know you need, and do what you say you will do. That's a great place to start to strengthen your voice.

As you're ready, move into areas you find more challenging, like setting boundaries in relationships because you need honesty or trust. Or telling your boss you want a raise because you value your contribution. Or starting new relationships with people using their own voices toward a contented life, just like you.

You know what you need, and you will know where you need to express it. The more you trust your truth and step out to speak it, the stronger your voice will become. The stronger your voice becomes, the stronger and more healed you become.

It will take time to feel as though using your voice is as easy. There will always be circumstances that challenge you to dig deeper for more self-understanding in order to speak with your head held high.

But instead of looking outside for validation or direction on how to do that, you'll be looking inside.

And you'll always have your "Me."

---

Dianna Leeder, CPCC, is a Certified Co-Active Life Coach, and a Certified Confidence Coach through the American Confidence Institute. Her entire career has been based on helping women use their voices to gain strength and align to themselves and their needs, currently as owner of Crave More Life Coaching. She is a healer of broken spirits, a teacher of self-reliance, and a partner in getting your voice and your life back. Find more and follow her blog at https://cravemorelife.com/.

In her other "aligned" time, Dianna has been married to the same guy, like forever. Family means so much, and she is blessed with three amazing grandkids who she intentionally creates her relationships with and coaches them to do the same. When she's not hanging with the family she might be traveling, designing great space, warm water swimming or leisurely biking, savoring good food and good wine, or connecting with the energies of loved ones who have left this world.

# CHAPTER 23

# Being Aloha
## A Way of Accessing Nature

### BY SARAH NANI WILLIAMS PsyD

## My Story

In November of 1979, when I was five years old, I remember sitting on the floor as my mother brushed my hair in our apartment in Kuwait. She received a sudden, disturbing phone call from my father. I overheard my mother ask, "What? You have to work late?" Her voice became shaky as I heard her say, "There's a threat of an attack? It's not safe for us here? I'll pack the bags so we can leave as soon as possible. Please come home soon. Be safe." As she hung up the phone, a dark cloud of anxiety and tension enveloped my mother, and I felt it encroaching on my space as well. That night I slept with my mother, falling asleep despite the intense fear that surrounded us. In the middle of the night, I was startled awake by my father picking me up. I took comfort in the warmth of his arms before he returned me to my bed, and I fell back asleep. Before the sun rose, I was once again woken up by my father lifting me out of bed. As my family walked out of the house, I remember being in my father's arms and waving goodbye to my Christmas presents that were in the closet that I knew I was not going to see for a long time, if ever. In that moment we were surrounded by fear and uncertainty around if and when we would ever return to our home. At this time, my family and I were acting from a place of survival.

There are a lot of experiences and stressors in life that can lead us to living from a place of survival. When I was six years old, we moved back to the United States, and I spent the next two decades going through school. While pursuing my education, I attended thirteen different schools and lived in eight different cities. This period definitely had turbulent times, including being teased, struggling with schoolwork, and changing schools often. I remember the kids teasing me on the playground in New York in fifth grade after I read out loud in class saying, "You are from Mars," and them laughing at me. When I was in college in New Orleans, and I was finally diagnosed with a learning disability, I jumped for joy. I felt immense relief to finally have a name for why things were so difficult and cumbersome in school. With that diagnosis, I then understood that my brain just processed information differently, and I could start the process of beginning to let go of the tapes in my head that were constantly saying: *I am dumb. I am stupid. I am lazy.*

Even with my diagnosis and the accommodations I was given, taking academic tests was still no small feat. I completed my doctoral program in Chicago without reading books and having written assignments transcribed. A particular memory that stands out for me is when I had a take-home exam in graduate school, and the deadline to turn it in was right around the corner. I had ten hours of assistance scheduled to help me for the day at the Blind Services Association. Shortly after arriving and starting to work, the lights and power at the Association went out, and it closed. I started panicking about how to meet the deadline after losing the ten hours of assistance. Three of the elderly gentlemen that had been scheduled to help me approached and stated that they were still willing to work with me. My school was only two blocks away. Together we walked there, rolling suitcases full of books down the street. When we arrived, the power at the school was intermittent. Riding up the elevator, we did not know if we were going to get stuck between floors. We ended up working for two hours together in the 'fishbowl' room because it had the most natural light. One gentleman read to me, one helped with the bibliography, and the other one acted as the supervisor. I was so grateful that these gentlemen stuck with me. It was an unforgettable afternoon, and in the end, I aced the exam.

Many of my experiences in school involved problem solving, and I ultimately completed my doctoral degree after six years of graduate study. During this time, my life felt chaotic. I lived from a place of moving through challenge after challenge, having to overcome hurdle after hurdle. It felt like a constant struggle and an uphill battle. I felt that I was not good enough, and I needed to expend a lot of effort and energy to prove myself. The way I coped with these times was to develop a hard exterior focused on goal attainment to hide my interior world of fragmented pieces and feelings of defeat. During the times when I wanted to quit my doctoral program or give up, I reminded myself, *I am doing this for the children and clients that I will help in the future.*

There are moments in our lives that change our perception. A week before my thirtieth birthday, I can still feel myself walking in front of my friend in my Chicago office, as I opened the door to sit on the porch with her. I saw the sky, a shining bright blue with no clouds. My eyes still on the sky, I heard her say, "I am taking a Hawaiian class," and without missing a beat, I heard myself say, "I am too." In that moment, my entire body and mind shifted. I clearly experienced the profound expansion and flow I could live in. Immediately I said, "Wait! What is that?!" I felt expansion, freedom, connection, and apprehension all in that moment. This experience opened a pathway to how I could live the rest of my life. I had always felt a deep bodily connection to intuition and forces I did not yet have words for. In that moment I tapped into this space. I would later discover that this was me experiencing aloha.

We experience times in our lives when our notion of what is possible is expanded. In my first Hawaiian class with kumu (teacher) Rick Pono'uhane Ho'okuakua Vrenios, my understanding of home and family was deepened. The seeds were planted for me to be able to access acceptance within myself and from my external environment and community. This class started me on my journey into learning about and understanding the healing arts and old ways of a family lineage of medical kahuna that traces back thousands of years. I have come to learn how important the old ways are. They focus on connection, unity, community, observation, and learning through experience. Things are simple. *Yes, and not always easy.* Over the years, when the lineage holder, my primary kumu, Ed Kaleolani Spencer, would teach in the old ways and tell a 'talk story' in class, he spoke with a flow and ease that was dynamic. Hearing him was like watching a hula performance, and the words had strength, direction, grace, and movement. His presence, awareness, and integration inspired me. I embarked on the journey to embody these concepts for myself. This started with me mimicking this behavior the best that I could in order to incorporate these elements into my way of being in the world. I began to notice the sacredness that surrounded me constantly and started to see how I could begin to incorporate ceremony into my everyday life.

In the Hawaiian lineage, students are given Hawaiian names based on the essence of their nature. I was given my name eleven years ago. Sitting in an office in Chicago with Kaleolani, my kumu, at sunset, the sunlight streamed in through the window, creating a sparkly reddish and purple cloud. We both went silent. I experienced this very tangible, hazy cloud and felt a whoosh of clarity and excitement through my body that brought me a sense of expansion. Looking off into the distance, Kaleolani said, "That's interesting, I just heard your Hawaiian name." My kumu wrote it down on a piece of paper and handed it to me. "*Kawahinekō-makaninani*, the woman who glides on the gentle breezes. This is your name." Being given this name started my process of learning to step into my power and embody my relationship with myself through the wind. Tuning into the wind puts a spotlight on what is going on internally and brings breath, freedom, and function. *I start mimicking the flow and the ease of the wind, which soothes my body. I allow myself to experience strength and boundlessness past the pain of my physical and emotional body.* My experience with the wind brings ease to help navigate the stressors of life.

There are times in our lives when listening allows us to tap into the grace and flow of life, and the pathway is clear. Every single person, interaction, thought, aspect of nature and experience up to this point culminated in preparing me for the opportunity to finally choose where I wanted to live in the world. My experiences with the Hawaiian lineage, culture, and healing practices had such a positive impact on my life that I felt deeply inspired to move to Maui. When I arrived, the presence of aloha enveloped me, and I was excited to finally create a home with community. Living in Hawaii, my life became more integrated, with nature and ceremony being an integral part of my daily life.

When I experience the stress and mundaneness of survival or task-oriented expression, I now tap into my resources, which allows me to access and shift back into the flow of aloha. When I experience stress, my nervous system can get agitated, and my skin gets flushed. If this happens, I often get frustrated with the difficulty presented by my learning disability, and shut down further. I have learned to connect with nature, elements, and aloha to support myself in these instances. The other day when this happened, I looked outside my window and saw the ocean. Here is what occurred as I became present with nature:

*I notice the waves. The rhythmic quality of the waves. I choose to follow the lullaby of the waves. All the colors and the light remind me of a tapestry. Each part has its own place. It brings a sense of calm and ease. Everything has its place. I can be safe and have a strong foundation to move forward. I am slowing down. I feel a softness in my breath. I can feel the rhythm in my body starting to mimic the fluidity that I see in the ocean. This gives me a sense of confidence and strength.*

Turning back to my daily life, my body is calmer, my thoughts are running smoothly, the inflammation and frustration in my body decreases. This sense of ease, safety, and consistency makes the stressors easier to navigate.

I invite you to stop, observe, and decide which resources you choose to bring into your life in a conscious and purposeful way. Nature and many resources are all around. They invite us to shift out of the survival and task-oriented modes and connect to the flow of aloha.

## The Tool

Let's start this tool with an introduction of aloha. The word 'aloha' has many different meanings. This is because the Hawaiian language was originally an oral tradition. Sounds, movements, and images came first, which were then translated into the written word. Being a pictorial language, words have layers of meaning. Aloha means hello, goodbye, and love. It can be literally translated as the joyful sharing of life and presence of breath, and yet it also means so much more. Aloha invites us to live in integrity and understand that there are no impossibilities.

These are the principles of aloha:

Ala-watchful alertness
Lokahi- unity
'Oia'i'o- truthful honesty
Ha'aha'a- humility
Ahonui- patient perseverance

Living in aloha, we increase the flow of love and joy in ourselves. We have the opportunity to shed fears and self-doubt and increase our level of safety, confidence, spontaneity, and creativity. We are able to embody presence, fullness, and participation in this rich and full way of living. This creates ease in our relationships and allows us to give from a place of overflow.

I am excited to share this tool that invites aloha. Let's begin. Turn off your phone; this time is for you. Take a couple of minutes and find a place you can observe nature. Walk outside or look out your window. I am going to walk you through an example of this tool with a tree. See which tree catches your attention. Find a tree with leaves or a palm tree, depending on where you live. Take a few breaths in through your nose and out your mouth. This rhythmic breathing will reset your nervous system to a relaxed state. Feel your body and the connection it has to the ground or chair. This will bring your attention to presence. Then look at the tree. In the aloha way, we will first say thank you to the tree for its presence in this moment to embrace the connection. Say something like, "Thank you tree, please partner with me for this experience." Observe what you see: the shapes, the colors, the textures, the movements that catch your attention. Notice if any of these qualities resonate in your body. See if the visual stimulates any part of your body when you are looking at these qualities in the tree. Start moving like the tree or its branches. Can you feel that kind of movement somewhere in your body? Allow the movement you see in the leaves to ripple through your body. Where does it go, and what do you feel? What else do you feel in your body when you are mimicking the tree? Are there sensations? Where are they? What do they feel like? When experiencing your body, what understandings bubble to the surface? Keep mimicking the tree, and pick a few leaves or a palm branch. What do you notice? What does this bring up that can be used in this moment? What rises to the surface while seeing and being part of the nature and aloha that is available? Take a few moments to be with your experience and let it integrate. Express gratitude for the tree. Celebrate the insights and clarity that you are taking with you. Remember, you can observe, experience nature, and access aloha at any time.

You'll find an audio version of this tool at:
https://lehualanicenter.org/aloharesources.

As my understanding of aloha deepens, my experience of this simple tool grows and expands. Yours can too. Here is an example of what I receive from nature now:

Looking at the palm tree outside my window, I start giggling. *The tips of the leaves rustling in the wind bring to mind thoughts of little hands playing the keys of a piano as they playfully dance in the wind. I can hear the melody of the leaves—a sense of creativity and lightheartedness sway through my body. I feel a fullness in my heart and a sense of childlike joy. The movement of the leaves reminds me of unity and how all things work together. The ease of movement flows through my body and reminds me that I don't need to take myself so seriously. I am drawn to go with the flow and ease and infuse humor along the way. One of the leaves is reaching out a hand and inviting me to come play. I think it is time to go paint.*

Turning back to my present life, my body is energized, excited, and playful. I am aware of the desire to nourish myself with self-care. This allows me to move forward in my day with a renewed sense of joy, creativity, grace, and playfulness. The reflections I received allow me to see through distractions and provide a reference point. This tool brings us to a place where aloha and nature meet.

When you use this tool, get creative. You can draw your observations, write them down, or use movement to express yourself. You are part of nature. Use whatever you would like. The sky, trees, bushes, rivers, ocean, plants, flowers, rain, and snow falling are some possible examples. This tool starts with ho'opili, which is the Hawaiian word for 'mimicking.' It is how they were taught in the old ways. Use the same routine. Stop, ask, observe, participate, integrate, and celebrate the experience. This is a simple tool that is used over and over again by beginners and masters. It is the foundation for physical, emotional, and spiritual healing.

Sarah Kawahinekōmakaninani Williams PsyD is the director of the Lehualani Center, a licensed clinical psychologist, a published author, and a Hawaiian Energetics Master Level Practitioner. She received her Doctorate in Psychology (PsyD) from the Illinois School of Professional Psychology in Chicago and has successfully worked with children, adolescents, adults, and families since 1995. She is certified in Child and Adolescent Gestalt Play Therapy through the West Coast Institute and provides Gestalt Play Therapy trainings for colleagues. Dr. Sarah is EMDR certified and has extensive experience working with children and adults with trauma. For more information on Dr. Sarah's psychology practice, please visit: http://sarahwilliamspsyd.com/.

Since 2005 Dr. Sarah has been studying Hawaiian Energetics, which originate from the ancient wisdom of the medical Kahuna. At the Lehualani Center, she provides Hawaiian Energetics treatments and Hawaiian Cranial Sacral Therapy. During a healing session, the creative force of Mana, the four elements (Fire, Water, Air, Earth) and aloha, are combined in a way and flow specifically for your healing. Physical, emotional, energetic, and spiritual healing is available for your renewal, equilibrium, and a sense of wellbeing.

Dr. Sarah has presented numerous times throughout the United States and Canada at schools and conferences. Many of these presentations discussed anxiety, depression, embodied presence, learning disabilities, and Attention-Deficit/Hyperactivity Disorder (ADHD) in adults and children. She co-presented a Hawaiian Energetics lecture and gave treatments at the Autism Today Conference in Vancouver, Canada, with her kumu, Ed Kaleolani Spencer. Dr. Sarah has presented lectures and workshops on "Living Aloha" in Hawaii, Illinois, and Utah.

The Lehualani Center is a nonprofit organization rooted in Ancient Hawaiian teachings, which is a worldwide ohana focused on increasing joy, authenticity, and harmony in our lives and communities. The Lehualani Center has started a project of doing fifty aloha events in the next five years. Check out https://lehualanicenter.org/ to find the schedule for the next event. Join like-minded people in spreading aloha across the world.

You'll find an audio version of this tool and a reading of the entire chapter at:

https://lehualanicenter.org/aloharesources.

# CHAPTER 24

# Visualization

## Train Your Brain and Your Pain

### BY LAURA FUREY, CHC, M.S. CANDIDATE

## My Story

When I was in college, I got sick with mononucleosis. Following this, I slowly started to become plagued with illnesses over the years. I became a medical anomaly from all aspects: from being diagnosed with conditions with no treatments, to severe hormone issues that had no clear cause, all the way to having idiopathic osteoporosis at the age of twenty. I started to watch my life slip away and my body slowly fall apart while I gathered almost twenty diagnoses without answers. I soon became bedridden and couldn't walk or feed myself. On the worst days, I couldn't roll over in bed without assistance. I had thrown myself into getting better until the point you could argue that it was an addiction that had taken over my life. It only made sense to me because I needed to be well again. Why could wanting to be well again so badly be a bad thing? I tried every conventional route imaginable. I tried the intensive therapy route. The nutritional. The spiritual. They all gave me life experience and wisdom but made little difference in my overall picture. Little did I know, spending my days in constant resistance and desperation wasn't helping me in the slightest.

When it came to the power of the mind-body connection, I'd tried all of the techniques out there. The list included: thinking positively, visualization, changing your thoughts, prayer/meditation, and that long list of things we're often advised to explore when all Hell is breaking loose in our lives. I'd even have those deep, profound, spiritual moments and would find that amazing space of "everything is going to be okay," and "I'm going to be well," only to have it fly out the window when life and my body would throw another curveball. The depths of darkness I experienced were indescribable as my life withered down to a minute fraction of the one I once knew it as. By the time I was 24, I was a 79-pound bag of bones that was slowly dying (literally) in front of my friends' and family's eyes while everyone, including myself, watched helplessly.

I ended up eventually having a near-death experience in the summer of 2014, which landed me in the hospital for quite a long time. Conventional medicine saved my life after I had rejected it for the last few years. I had given up on it as I had reached a point of feeling completely failed and somewhat mistreated by the system (look up the average time it takes a woman to get taken seriously by a doctor). The way medicine had failed me and also saved me when it came down to life or death, taught me an important life lesson. I would learn to carry the importance of balance in everything going forward. A combination of conventional emergency interventions, and my own rock bottom helped me to be able to make the decision I wanted to live, and that my happiness was no longer dependent on my physical limitations. I refer to that as my enlightenment moment. I know I will carry that with me for the rest of my life.

While I'm very grateful, and always will be, that medical intervention saved my life, it did not get me well. It got me functional enough to sit in a wheelchair and quasi be a "participant" in life with daily assistance. The survival time had passed, and the real work of healing began. It required the same balance I learned to value. It required surrendering, trusting, faith, and patience. It required learning to go with the flow (even if the current flow was suffering) rather than against it. It required seeing the big picture rather than the small day-to-day details. It required a constant overhaul of my beliefs and values and rebuilding everything I thought I knew to be true. This included rebuilding what I thought my identity was. It required going through, rather than around, many emotions of pain, sadness, and anger to come out on the other side. It required forgiveness (or letting go). It required perseverance and tenacity, as there would be numerous sick periods (blips as I like to say), broken bones, and injuries. There would also be a lot of moments of pure bliss, presence, joy, and gratitude. They all had to be equally welcomed.

There are many doctors, healers, physical therapists, and coaches I would have to credit for their aid on the journey, including my therapist, but one of the most profound turning points was discovering neuroplasticity. Norman Doidge's book, *The Brain's Way of Healing,* will always be one of my Aha moments. I feel blessed to have been able to tell him directly at a conference a year ago. When I discovered the concept of neuroplasticity and its application for healing, I started to understand where my potential for healing lay. Many chronic conditions can be linked back to experiencing an event that triggered it (physical, emotional, environmental, or a combination). Over time, new neural connections start being made, and these pathways start to become the norm. It soon becomes the learned pathway, and even though the illness, stressor, injury, etc. has passed or should have healed, the brain is now stuck in this faulty wiring (Schubiner & Betzold, 2019). This is an example where neuroplasticity, or the brain's ability to change, may have caused a hindrance, but can also come to the rescue. We first have to know how we should go about making changes; it's typically a multi-faceted approach.

## The Tool

Visualization has been around for longer than we can remember. It's touted from the tool to achieve the life you want, to the one for practicing a new skill you want to acquire, to the solution to all your pains and woes. I tend to use the phrase, "It's really that simple, but it's also not," because we are these complicated things called human beings walking through this complicated process called human life. As we continue to evolve and advance our knowledge and understanding, it's becoming more evident that the process of visualization has science to back it up. It took me a few years, but I eventually found the amazing power of this tool as one part of my toolbox on my healing journey. When I teach stress management tools, it's one that receives the most feedback in terms of effectiveness, mostly because it's so simple, yet so powerful. Every time we start to be pulled into the illness/pain condition (this includes chronic stress), we want to give the brain new input to work with.

Go ahead and close your eyes. You can choose to imagine whatever makes you feel good, but I usually recommend choosing something that makes you feel joyful, peaceful, safe, and relaxed. This can be your favorite place to be, a scene in nature, something you have lived, or something you could imagine living. I want you to pull this scene up and live it with all five senses. What do you see? Smell? Touch? Hear? Feel?

If you're someone who might get lost in their head, say it aloud. I should be able to just as strongly feel your visualization as you do if you were to say it aloud, describing everything with your five senses. I want to highlight that you need to really bring up the FEELING of this scene. How do you feel physically, emotionally, spiritually? When you come back to the room, you should feel like you just got to live an experience without ever having physically left. You should notice even the slightest shift in well being. It's not about going from a ten to zero, but even a one-point shift is how changes are slowly made.

I will walk you through one of mine now, although I suggest trying to read it aloud. I am walking to my favorite rock in my favorite park. It's a beautiful autumn day. Daisy (my dog) is running in zig zags in front of me, constantly making sure I'm still behind her. I can feel the sun beating down on my back, and I can smell the ocean air. I see a couple of small boats on the horizon line. I'm completely present, and as we reach the rock, I slowly climb on top of it. I take my shoes off and feel the heat and the rock beneath my feet. Daisy looks out into the water. I take a seat and feel my butt held by the rock beneath me. I look out into the vast ocean and feel small at this moment. I connect to that feeling that I'm only one small piece of this vast universe. Everything naturally slows down in my body: my breath, my heart rate, and I feel extreme peace. At this moment, everything else in the world falls away. I eventually lay back on the rock and feel the heat behind me and the sun coming down on me. I soak in the moment fully. Eventually, Daisy starts hitting me with her paw as her patience has expired. I slowly start to get up with a light and relaxed feeling in my body. I feel grounded in this moment. I move with a lightness, feeling the earth beneath my feet. Daisy starts to run ahead of me, still looking back to make sure I am following her. I take a look around and take more mental captures of the scenery and make my way back to the car.

I would probably embellish the details even more if actually doing the full visualization. As you can see, it's an extremely descriptive experience. Here's where many people go wrong, and this is very important. We are not working to change the symptom/discomfort in the moment. If it happens, great, but we are working to create a new connection in the brain, and that takes time. This is why I tend to suggest visualizations that make you feel peaceful and relaxed. I tend to choose this one often because it activates those feelings for me. I encourage these types of visualizations because learning these feelings as a new norm allows you to respond to uncomfortable things in this manner rather than waiting for uncomfortable things to pass to be able to access this state. So often we think, *I can't feel at peace or content unless "XYZ" happens.* We all do this in life, waiting for something better to come to dictate our happiness. This is why so many of us are living in a chronic stress response without even realizing it, only further ingraining these pathways.

As your brain has become so wired to a faulty wiring norm, it's important to understand the amount of repetition it will take to start to replace the old pathway. That said, if you want to choose something that's more exciting or energizing, go for it, but we're committed to the visualization itself having slow and long-lasting effects, and not necessarily an immediate grand change in the moment (though that *can* happen).

It is crucial to use positive language, always focusing on what you want to feel rather than on what you don't want. Examples: "I feel great in my body," vs. "I don't feel pain," or "I feel calm and relaxed," vs. "I don't feel anxious." Make sure to use present language. It sounds mind-boggling, but the brain doesn't differentiate greatly between an imagined experience and real experience (Doidge, 2017). When we look at some basic neuroscience, the reticular activating system (RAS) part of our brain is what goes to work in the visualization process. The RAS is constantly fielding input all day long because our brains literally can't take everything in. When you give it new things to look for, it will start to filter information to confirm this experience (Wilis, 2012). This is why our language choice is extremely powerful.

Repetition is also an important component that a lot of people tend to forget. Every single time you find yourself back in the condition (illness, pain, stress, anxiety, etc...), be it via the physical experience, or all the thought patterns around it, you want to activate a new response by using your visualization. It may feel tedious, but think about the number of times this old pathway has fired. Your job is to outdo that number! While we are playing catch up to that, you should be able to notice a shift in mood elevation as you keep doing them. The more we can help ourselves flow through rough moments, the more we turn off the internal stress response. Stay with the current moment of the experience of the visualization. Too often, we jump ship on the new state we're creating for ourselves when we constantly try to look to our current reality for validation. Be patient. Also, this tool is multi-faceted; it's a great tool to use at any moment, even for the day-to-day. Visualization is wonderful when dealing with a stressful event. Tune in to the feelings you want to activate. Live it while you say it. So many times, people enjoy doing it once or twice and then go into automatic pilot again. You want to activate parts of the brain to feel the experience and you want to do that often (Askenasy & Lehmann, 2013). In the beginning, when you're attempting to change a very ingrained pattern, you might be doing this fifty times a day! You will be amazed at how often you're actually caught back up in the condition.

I look back over the years of using this tool properly. I think about how everything I've visualized in the last few years has come to fruition; sometimes, it just took longer than I would have thought. It has allowed me to shift very unpleasant moments quickly to help me remember I have a choice in responding in a way that feels good. This is one tool in the box of neuroplasticity tips that has been an asset for healing so many of those long list of conditions. In my early healing years, it also helped me step out of the anxiety of trying to navigate the world with physical limitations and step into feelings of trust and peace. In fact, I have repeated it so often that I often only need to close my eyes and say a few sentences to create a physiological shift in my body. The greatest gift is it's given me a way to remember how to access the feeling of flow rather than resistance and stress. If there is one thing I would give myself advice on ten years ago: stop fighting so hard, your true power lies in presence and surrender to the current moment.

## REFERENCES

Askenasy, J., & Lehmann, J. (2013). Consciousness, brain, neuroplasticity. Frontiers in Psychology, 4. doi:10.3389/fpsyg.2013.00142

Doidge, N. (2017). The brain's way of Healing: Remarkable discoveries and recoveries from the frontiers of neuroplasticity. Brunswick, Victoria: Scribe.

Schubiner, H., & Betzold, M. (2019). Unlearn your pain: A 28-day process to reprogram your brain. Pleasant Ridge, MI: Mind

Body Publishing.

Wilis, J. (2012). Powerful!Classroom!Strategies! From! Neuroscience! Research! Retrieved June 14, 2020, from https://www.learningandthebrain.com/documents/WillisHandout.pdf

---

Laura Furey is a certified integrative health coach with her own coaching practice, A-HAH! Coaching. She works with clients all over the world struggling with chronic illness/pain, stress, and anxiety. She has a large focus on using the power of neuroplasticity and embodiment for healing and sustainable transformation. She is currently finishing up a master's in clinical mental health counseling to further facilitate the work with her clients as they explore the mind-body connection. Outside of coaching and studying, she lives with her best friend, a rescue dog named Miss Daisy. She is also fluent in Spanish and has a passion for the language. You can find her at www.ahahcoaching.com and/or www.facebook.com/ahahcoaching.

# CHAPTER 25

# Hiring a Guide
## Taking Your Health
## to the Next Level

### BY LAURA DI FRANCO, MPT

All the experts here agree that empowering you by giving you tools to treat yourself at home is one of the keys to healing. When you take responsibility for self-awareness, self-care, self-healing, and self-development, you are much more apt to feel good and stay feeling that way. We've experienced clients who take self-treatment to heart getting better faster, staying healthier in the long run, and really enjoying their lives to the fullest.

We also know many people need skilled assistance and guidance to feel better. The clients we come across are in all stages of physical, mental, and emotional dis-ease or dysfunction. Some need a quick tool and home program, while others require intensive or prolonged care. We all agree that having a guide on the journey is paramount to peak performance, whatever stage you're in.

When you have a guide, coach, or healer in your corner, you'll reach your goals faster, but more importantly, you'll have someone invested in your progress and healing, and you won't be doing it alone. Remember, that guide has been where you are, and has healed the layers you're going through. He or she is able to hold a healing space for you to do that same work. Holding a healing space for you means they've practiced a conscious presence, an ability to ground and center themselves, and an ability to energetically enhance your healing process. Conscious presence requires consistent practice. It's a practice that healers have worked for years to master. They've adopted a lifestyle that includes these skills and tools, so they can help others. They are special, amazing people.

This final note is to encourage you to seek out a guide if you feel like you're stuck, not making progress, feeling more hopeless than hopeful, or just can't consistently get your mindset to stay positive, open, or clear. We encourage you to explore different modalities and different guides, coaches, and practitioners. Find someone you vibe with and hire them to help you get to where you want to go.

Try asking: What else is possible for my healing today? Just asking yourself that question should help you feel hopeful. Sit with that question without straining to hear an answer. Allow yourself to meditate on the possibility.

Another great question to sit with, and/or journal about: What if there's something you haven't learned yet that could change everything?

We sit around and think we've read it all, done it all, and learned it all, and we stay resigned to our current mediocre physical, mental, emotional status because we think there are no alternatives or options left. I've been exploring healing and the vast array of healing modalities for an entire lifetime, and I'm here to tell you I won't have time to get to all the possibilities.

The point here is there are people out there who will help you heal. There's a guide out there waiting to teach you something you didn't even know existed and expose you to another level of hope you didn't realize you could feel. This book outlines dozens of those approaches. Some traditional. Some alternative. Some you may have never heard of. Some you may have heard of but never tried. It's time to explore!

It's our job as authentic healers, practitioners, and guides to facilitate a process of healing in you, connect you with your inner healer and power, and super-boost that power inside you. And we're good at it. Try us!

Please go back to the chapters that drew you in, piqued your interest, or had you feeling a little excited. Look up the amazing author there and read a little bit more about them on their website. You might even contact them to say thank you for their words, or set up a call with them to discuss what you learned. The authors I asked to be a part of this are cool like that; they want you to feel better, and they are open-hearted, skilled, and very aware and experienced healers. They thrive when you thrive. It's part of their mission, like it is mine, to help heal the world.

I hope you enjoyed this book. Even more than that, I hope you're getting into action with it, trying the exercises and tools, and getting some results! I'd love to hear how you're doing. Hop over to www. BraveHealer.com and send me a note! Remember, as an owner of this book you can have access to a private Facebook group where all the Ultimate Guide experts are hanging out and doing some live training! Claim your access here: https://lauradifranco.com/ultimate-self-healing/.

Lastly, I have a personal favor to ask. If you enjoyed this book and have a couple minutes to leave a review on Amazon, I'd greatly appreciate it. Your review helps others see our book, and it spreads the good vibes. Thank you!

Signing off now with a final wish for your best health. May you find what you need to thrive, mind, body, and soul.

With warrior love,
Laura

# A Rampage of Gratitude

Gratitude is the energy I wanted to purposefully end the book with, in hopes you'll read these last pages and imagine all the people in your own life you're grateful for, maybe even some of these fantastic authors!

This is more than acknowledging people for their help with this book, it's conjuring up energy we can take with us as we move forward into our purpose and mission of helping the world heal. Appreciation is the energy of manifestation! It's a magical, foundational mindset that everything good is born from.

So, amazing reader, thank you for being here! For being open to learning. And for exploring this fascinating world of healing with me and all of the authors here. You are powerful, and have limitless potential to heal yourself! Step into your power, use the tools, ask more questions, and adopt a lifestyle of learning. That's how you'll continue to evolve and feel the most peace, happiness, and health in the future. I'm so grateful to be walking alongside you on this journey.

To my authors, the badassery you've laid down on these pages is beyond what I'd hoped for. In the many conversations I had with you during the writing phase of your chapters you gave me your trust, and allowed me to inspire you, even though you may have been unsure. You believed me when I told you how important your authentic stories are and you told them, without apology, and with a stupendous courage and generosity. Thank you for that. Thank you for saying yes to this project! And thank you for stepping up to teach what you know and gift our readers with your unique expertise, knowledge and skills. I'm so honored to be in your company.

To our book designer, Christy Collins, thank you for stepping up to make this book shine. I feel super grateful to know you and to have found someone who really understands my Brave Healing message. Find Christy on Facebook at Constellation Book Services.

To our front-cover artist, Mandy McMahan, whoa girl, this artwork embodies healing. Thank you so much for being a part of this project and giving this book its face for the world. Find Mandy on Instagram y'all: https://www.instagram.com/mandymcmahan/

To all our friends, family, colleagues, acquaintances and book launch team members who supported us during the writing, publishing, launching and promoting of this project, thank you so much for your support, love, words of encouragement, and purchases. This village is badass!

# Join the AUTHOR TEAM for the next Ultimate Guide to Self-Healing book!

Brave Healer Productions is now accepting applications to be part of our next book!

You're a healer...
...and a business owner, and you're ready to share your message with the world in a bigger way!

Contributing a chapter to this powerful collaborative project is much more than just having your name on a book.

It's about being part of a community of healthcare entrepreneurs who are changing the world with their brave words and tools.

Each author shares their story, and teaches an effective self-healing tool in their chapter. Authors then have opportunities to do live training, podcast interviews, and business development activities as a part of the Brave Healer Productions family.

We can't wait to hear your story!

Submit your application today!
https://lauradifranco.com/ultimate-guide-project/

"All I can say is, if you have a book inside you, a message you want to gift the world, or a healing business you want to grow, there is no one better than Laura Di Franco, and Brave Healer Productions. She and her team will guide you through all the stages, from concept to writing to getting your book into the hands of your readers. She genuinely wants to bring health and healing to the world we all live in. And she delivers big time."

–Dr. Shelley Astrof, Author of The Knower Curriculum

"It's one thing to have a process that will help a book become successful. It's a whole other thing to create success from a place of holding sacred space and unconditional warrior love for every person she works with to step into their capacity for brilliance. My heart is grateful for the innumerable ways Laura has created for authors to connect with readers."

–Sharon Carne, Director of Training and Development, Sound Wellness

"Laura Di Franco is a master at helping your work take flight and land with your target audience. She has a unique ability to help you draw out your good ideas, and her experience in the world of writing quickly moves ideas to action. Laura has no shortage of ideas for your success and will give you more than you could imagine possible. Trust her to land your words!"

–Dr. Erika Putnam, DC, RYT 500

Submit your story idea here:
https://lauradifranco.com/ultimate-guide-project/

# OTHER BOOKS BY LAURA DI FRANCO

*The Ultimate Guide to Self-Healing Techniques, Volume 1*

*Living, Healing and Tae Kwon Do, a Memoir to Inspire Your Inner Warrior*

*Brave Healing, a Guide for Your Journey*

*Your High Vibe Business, a Strategic Workbook for Badass Entrepreneurial Success*

*Warrior Love, a Journal to Inspire Your Fiercely Alive Whole Self*

*Warrior Joy, a Journal to Inspire Your Fiercely Alive Whole Self*

*Warrior Soul, a Journal to Inspire Your Fiercely Alive Whole Self*

*Warrior Dreams, a Journal to Inspire Your Fiercely Alive Whole Self*

*Warrior Desire, Love Poems to Inspire Your Fiercely Alive Whole Self*

Your words will change the world when you're brave enough to share them. Your fear of not-good-enough is boring. What if the thing you're still a little afraid to share is exactly what someone needs to hear to change, or even save their life? It's time to be brave.

–Laura Di Franco

Made in the USA
Middletown, DE
14 September 2020